P9-DDW-257

He Speaks
the Word of
GOD

ALLAN R. BROADHURST

He Speaks the Word of GOD

*A Study of the Sermons
of Norman Vincent Peale*

Prentice-Hall Inc., Englewood Cliffs, N.J.

HE SPEAKS THE WORD OF GOD: *A Study of the Sermons of Norman Vincent Peale,* by Allan R. Broadhurst

Printed in the United States of America
38433-T

Acknowledgments

It is an author's privilege to acknowledge the personal debts he has incurred while doing his research, and although it is not possible for me to list them all, I record with pleasure my chief creditors. Especial thanks goes to Dr. Donald Ecroyd of the Department of Speech, Michigan State University, who was always available, offering criticism and guidance as it was needed. Messrs. Jack Prather and Jim Clark assisted greatly in the programing of the theme material for use in the Michigan State University Mystic computer. To my wife, Mary, goes all my appreciation and gratitude; for this book is as much her contribution as it is mine.

Contents

*He Speaks
the Word of*
GOD

Chapter 1

Studying Dr. Peale

In 1932 Dr. Norman Vincent Peale delivered a guest sermon at the Marble Collegiate Church in New York City and was thereafter invited to take over the dwindling congregation. He accepted and thus obtained the leadership of the oldest chartered church in New York (1696), located in the heart of the metropolis, in the shadow of the Empire State Building.

Today, Dr. Peale preaches weekly to a capacity congregation and is recognized as one of the most influential Protestant preachers on the contemporary American scene. Fame did not come to him overnight, nor on the basis of one or two highly publicized sermons. Rather, it was (and is) based on a long period of speaking openly and with a unique point of view. As a writer, preacher, and public speaker, Dr. Peale has gradually emerged a person with great influence.

But the road to the national limelight has not been one of total glory. Like all other leaders of past and present, Dr. Peale has made enemies as well as friends. His critics have gone so far as to condemn his sermons and books as a perversion of Christianity. They have labeled him the leader of the new "cult of reassurance," or "cult of positive thinkers." The accusations of some of the critics stem probably from chance reading, the passion of emotionalism, and misguided opinion. However, many of the critics are sincere scholars who speak with the authority of the church behind them. But despite his critics, Dr. Peale receives weekly from people around the world thousands of letters bearing testimony of their loyalty to him.

In view of the controversial nature of the public image presented by Dr. Peale, the central purpose of this book is to analyze the content of his preaching. In a more specific sense, this study will be devoted to a thematic analysis of the sermons of Dr. Norman Vincent Peale. By means of the detailed quantification of themes, an effort will be made in this study to determine what Dr. Peale said and the frequency with which he said it. Answers, then, will be sought to the following questions:

(A)   What themes were advanced by Dr. Peale in his Sunday sermons at the Marble Collegiate Church?

(B)   How often did these themes appear?

(C)   What themes, determined by thematic quantification, constitute the basic theology of Dr. Peale?

(D)   What patterns, types, or clusters of agreement can be found among the themes present in Dr. Peale's sermons?

The foregoing questions are regarded as the primary purpose of this study. Also of importance in analyzing the preaching of Dr. Peale will be a consideration of his growth and development as a public speaker, and his ideas concerning speech making.

Dr. Peale has not always followed the practice of writing out in advance, or recording his sermons. Therefore, this study will be limited to an analysis of the sermons currently available. Dr. Peale's sermons are now recorded each Sunday, and with no apparent rationale for selection some are then printed by the Foundation for Christian Living, Pawling, New York.

As Pastor of Marble Collegiate Church in New York City, the Reverend Dr. Norman Vincent Peale is possibly the most highly publicized of metropolitan ministers. He occupies an important position in national church leadership and is well known to the public through his radio lectures, *Art of Living,* which have been heard on a national network for more than a decade. His dozen books have sold many millions of copies; the most famous, *The Power of Positive Thinking,* has sold 2,300,000 in various hard cover editions. In addition, he has several syndicated newspaper columns which appear daily and weekly, along with articles appearing from time to time in many current magazines. Also, his "Sermon Publications" are distributed monthly throughout the United States to a mailing list of over 400,000 people.

Any study of such a man would seem to be justified in view of his popularity, and the possibility of the study's potential contribution to a better understanding of contemporary preaching. It is felt by the author that Dr. Peale's sermons represent a larger sample of his thinking than his books; that is why the sermons were chosen for analysis.

This type of thematic analysis will enable us to apply a congruity rating between the content of Dr. Peale's message and the public image he presents, and can possibly serve as a guide for future studies where the content of materials is compared to a public image.

In general, the sources used include the current books, articles, and selected sermons of Dr. Norman Vincent Peale. Dr. Peale has expressed a spirit of cooperation in assisting "to the best of my ability" in the research for this study. Additional sources will include speech books, dissertations, social psychology texts, and texts in the field of communication theory.

This analysis is divided into two main parts. The first part is a historical study of Dr. Peale's development as a public speaker. The second section is a quantitative analysis of his sermon themes. In this section the themes are defined, analyzed, and interpreted.

The method to be employed in the second part of this study will involve six procedural steps in thematic analysis: (1) selection of materials, (2) designation of categories, (3) thematic definitions, (4) coding procedure, (5) reliability testing, and (6) method of tabulation.

Both parts of the study are necessary in order to account for the phenomenon of Dr. Peale's tremendous public influence.

Chapter 2

The Growth of Dr. Peale as a Speaker

A biography of Dr. Norman Vincent Peale has already been written and published. It is, therefore, not necessary to rewrite the life of Dr. Peale. The purpose of this chapter is to focus attention on those aspects of Dr. Peale's life which seem the most relevant to his development as a speaker and speech writer.

Norman Vincent Peale was born on May 31, 1898, in Bowersville, Ohio, a small rural town located in the southwestern section of the state. His father was the town's Methodist minister, and his mother had a talent for organization as well as a flair for public speaking. In his later years, Dr. Peale often reflected back on the tremendous enthusiasm possessed by his mother.

> . . . she was one of the most enthusiastic persons I ever knew. She got an enormous thrill out of the most ordinary events. She had the ability, in a marked manner, to see romance and glory in everything.[1]

She particularly enjoyed the religious conferences held at "Lakeside." It was there that the family heard the wonderful and exciting tales of foreign missionaries and of the exotic lands in which they administered the word of God. It was there, too, that

15

laymen were encouraged to enter public speaking contests, and Mrs. Peale emerged the winner in more than one.

By virtue of his position as one of the town ministers, Dr. Peale's father, Clifford Peale, was looked to as a man of moral purpose and conviction. Besides his many duties in the pulpit, he was frequently called on by the townsfolk to speak at civic functions. In fact, he delivered a Memorial Day oration the day before Norman was born.

As a boy, young Norman looked to his father as the embodiment of strength and leadership. "The fact that in church his father led the congregation and spoke with authority enhanced the aura." [2] Sunday after Sunday Norman witnessed the power religion had to change human lives and personalities. One of his earliest recollections was a service at which his father issued the familiar invitation to "come forward and surrender yourself to Jesus Christ." Up went one of the town "toughs," noted for his profane and hard-drinking ways. "He knelt at the altar while the congregation, hushed and awe-stricken, tried to help him with their prayers, tried to 'pray him through,' as the saying went." [3] The man did change his ways, and Norman, young as he was, "never forgot the radiance of the man's face or the feeling of power that came into the church, the mysterious power of religion to reach deep into the human heart and in an instant produce a miracle of personality regeneration." [4]

Dr. Peale lived always in a theological atmosphere, but this in no way meant that his life was destined to be somber or prosaic.

> [Mrs. Peale] . . . invented games that dramatized bed making or dishwashing. She recited poetry while she swept or dusted. She kept the house full of fun. . . .
>
> Clifford Peale's sense of humor included the capacity to laugh at himself. On the back of a rather glum photograph that showed him wearing a formidable plug hat he wrote, "Of course, if a man has a grouch like this, he ought not have his

picture taken. If he *insists,* this is certainly what he deserves!" Another snapshot, partially light-struck, showed him with a sort of nimbus in the general area of his head. "Note the halo!" he wrote gleefully, "A trifle premature!" [5]

Dr. Peale loved his father dearly. To him, Clifford Peale was the embodiment of love. "He had no hatred in his heart; . . . He could be firm sometimes, but never mean." [6]

Dr. Peale was a bright child, with a better than average ability to memorize. His mind was retentive, and focused on details which were quickly passed over and forgotten by others. He was sensitive and painfully shy, however, and "a sharp word could reduce him to gloom." [7] His parents, being extrovertive by training if not by birth, felt that this shyness and self-consciousness was definitely a handicap to be overcome.

Dr. Peale recalls spending his summers, as a youth, with his grandparents in a little town in southern Ohio. In the backyard was a wonderful barn. In that town it was the custom of the minister to make regular calls among the people of his parish. Since the visits were long, it gave the women a chance to let the minister sample their cooking, and it gave the men a chance to talk over the problems of the day. In addition, there was the custom of showing off the children by making them speak pieces for the minister.

> I got so that whenever the minister came I was unavoidably absent. I can remember my uncle coming around the barn where I lurked and taking me by the ear. "Norman," he said, "I am ashamed of you. You are a disgrace to the family. The minister is here and you haven't been in to speak to him." He led me by the ear, stood me in front of the minister and told me to speak my piece; which I did—something about the boy stood on the burning deck.[8]

This showing off of one's children was not always confined to the visit of the local minister. Often Norman's parents would call upon their bashful boy to recite a poem to an admiring circle of friends or relatives. On these occasions Dr. Peale had to be dragged from his hiding place to the living room, "where, like an early Christian being thrown to the lions, he was ordered to speak his piece. . . ." [9]

Dr. Peale's shyness was probably due, at least in part, to three influences upon his life. First, because his father was a Methodist minister, everyone expected him to be a perfect-little-angel at all times. The standards set for him were much higher than those set for his playmates. In order to camouflage his sensitiveness about being a preacher's son, he would sometimes do stunts like smoking cigarettes or racing his father's automobile.

A second influence contributing to his shyness was his size. He was short and extremely thin—always smaller than the other boys his age. Even as a young minister in his mid-twenties, Dr. Peale weighed only 126 pounds. Comments were frequently made by his parishioners that "we ought to take you home and fatten you up."

Then, too, Norman was always comparing himself to his brother Bob, two years younger. From the very start, Bob was the more rugged, the more athletic of the two. He was tough, aggressive, self-assured, ready for a fight, and endowed with a competitive instinct. Though Norman also had the desire to excel, he did not have his brother's heft and physique, and this troubled him.

Despite the physical difference in her two sons Mrs. Peale had equal ambitions for them both. Over and over again she would tell them, "You've got to love life. You've got to read everything, study everything, be interested in everything. You've got to be citizens of the world." [10]

"Be somebody, Abe," the dying mother of Lincoln had said at the end of her own unhappy life. In a thousand ways, consciously or unconsciously, Anna Peale said the same thing to her own sons.

She tried to kindle their imagination with fairy tales and poetry. She thrilled them with *Hans Brinker and the Silver Skates,* and the immortal story of the lad who saved Holland by plugging with his finger the hole in the dike. She told them the tales she had heard her Irish father tell of elves and leprechauns and the strange blue lights that flickered over the bogs of Killarney. She dramatized the great triumphant stories of the Bible: David slaying Goliath, Gideon and his gallant three hundred, Joshua causing the trumpets to blow that sent the walls of Jericho crashing down.

She told them of boys who rose from obscurity to become great men. Hans Christian Andersen, for example, who sat in his Copenhagen garret, poor and unknown, and looked out at the moonlight silvering the water and said to himself, "Some day, Hans Christian Andersen, you will be the most famous man in all of Denmark!"

Inevitably, his ambition was stirred. He loved his mother, he wanted to please her, to win her approval with achievement. And there were times when he felt that, like Andersen, he would turn out to be a famous man, if not in Denmark, then at least in Ohio.[11]

In response to his mother's guidance, Dr. Peale's view of himself began to take shape in the midst of a paradox. On the one hand he wanted to please his mother—to become a person of ultimate importance—yet on the other hand his feelings of self-doubt, fear, timidity, and shyness stood in his way. "These shadowy Siamese twins were to be his constant companions until, years later, deepening spiritual experience made it possible for him to rise above his own doubts. . . ."[12]

Dr. Peale's early understanding of life was also affected by the religious and spiritual experiences which played a dominant part in the life of most towns in Ohio during the early years of the twentieth century. Revivals were held regularly and with enthusiasm, and the small town inhabitants anxiously awaited the coming of a great evangelist or other religious speaker. These men, successors to Dwight L. Moody and forerunners of Billy Graham, were judged by the fire and turbulence of their preaching and the number of their conversions. Depending on their success, the camp meetings sometimes lasted for several weeks.

"The emotional impact of these gatherings on small-town life was enormous. Not only was religious fervor 'revived,' but human lives and personalities were dramatically changed." [13] As a boy, Dr. Peale saw these effects take place. Since his father was a minister, he had first-hand experiences which left their imprint on his young and pliable mind.

Then, too, everyday religion ran like a steady current through the family. There was always grace before meals. In the evening the family gathered for prayers and Bible reading, followed by personal prayers at bedtime. A minister's home was always open to his parishioners, and visiting churchmen frequently stopped in for a talk or a meal. Inevitably, questions and answers were argued and propounded—vigorous conversation being the order of the day. As Mrs. Peale once said, "The whole world seemed to troop into our dining room." [14]

As a student in high school, Dr. Peale's grades were "above average," but neither he nor his brother showed signs of fulfilling their mother's exhortations to put scholarship ahead of everything else. Dr. Peale's first public speech was delivered in the auditorium of the Greenville, Ohio, High School, which he attended. Despite rehearsing endlessly in front of mirrors, and deliberately memorizing the speech word for word, panic seized him as he walked toward the platform.

When I stood up, I became literally stiff with fear. I couldn't get the first words out. In this embarrassed silence, a little girl in the front row giggled to her mother, "Gosh, look at his knees shake." That made me so angry that I found my voice and gave a spirited speech.[15]

As the author of Dr. Peale's biography points out, the "shaking knees" were significant. Not only did they prove that their owner cared about the impression he was making, but they hinted that he cared so desperately that only two alternatives were possible. "Either he would avoid public speaking entirely—like the little boy who once hid in the attic when he saw visitors coming. Or else he would conquer his fears and force himself to excel at it." [16]

Because of his physical size, he could not find recognition on the athletic field—though he did eventually make the high school track team.

> As time went on he began to see, dimly, that if he was going to make a mark anywhere, if he was going to "be somebody" as his mother wanted and accomplish something worth-while in life, he was going to have to do it with his head—and with his tongue.[17]

Many years later, in an interview with Eugene White and Clair Henderlider, Dr. Peale said:

> I doubt that anyone was ever less likely to become an effective speaker than I. I definitely was not endowed with superior linguistic skill. In fact, as a boy in Ohio, I was exceedingly shy and inarticulate. . . . Much of any man's life consists of attempts to overcome his shortcomings. My own difficulties with speech probably stimulated me to want to become a skilled speaker. As far back as I can remember, I wanted to grow up to be an orator. . . . I wanted to be a great political spellbinder and hold thousands of listeners magnetized. I even dreamed of becoming the governor of Ohio and of having my statue placed along with those of Garfield, McKinley, and Sherman on the Capitol grounds at Columbus.[18]

Young Norman, little by little, realized his ambition to become an effective speaker. In high school he won some fame as a debater while brother Bob's football ability began to be noticed. It was largely due to his speaking ability that Norman was also elected President of the Boys' Congress of Ohio, an organization of boys with similar religious backgrounds. The Ohio Boys' Congress numbered several thousand members and offered Norman his first real test in the area of leadership and speech-making. As president, he traveled throughout the state, acting as guest speaker at the conventions of the organization and presiding at business meetings.

After graduating from high school, young Norman decided to enter college. There was no selection of colleges available to him, for Clifford Peale, his father, knew that Ohio Wesleyan University was the inevitable choice for any Methodist minister's son in Ohio. Clifford Peale wanted his son to get the education which he, himself, was denied—thus Norman entered Ohio Wesleyan in the autumn of 1916.

In his freshman year at college, he found a new freedom, a life relatively free from the restrictions placed on him as a minister's son in a small rural town. Perhaps his grades are an indication of the freedom he enjoyed. For the first semester his grades did not show a single "A" or "B."

> The liberal arts course at Ohio Wesleyan required no mathematics and little science. It stressed English, Oratory, a certain amount of History with emphasis on Bible study and the History of Christianity, and Economics. It also called for a nodding acquaintance with at least one ancient and one modern language. Norman already had some knowledge of German, and he did well with Spanish and French, when he got around to them. But his grades in Greek were almost as dismal as his records in required gym, where he earned straight F's. The one

bright spot in his freshman record was the A he achieved in Oratory—for extemporaneous speaking.[19]

During the four years at Ohio Wesleyan, Dr. Peale took two courses in elocution under Professor Charles Newcombe, who was an outstanding speaker himself. As Dr. Peale later reported:

> In these classes we got no practice in preparing original speeches, but spent our time delivering declamations. New-combe stressed communication of ideas and emotions; so the classes were not so artificial as they might seem.[20]

But Dr. Peale still suffered from the shyness that had plagued him throughout his younger years. This self-consciousness was particularly evident if he was called upon, unannounced, to recite in class. He was so bent on making the best impression possible, that he became stiff, unnatural, and paralyzed with fear. In a sermon delivered some forty years later Dr. Peale stated that as a student at Ohio Wesleyan:

> I was, without any doubt, the shyest, most retiring boy who ever lived in the state of Ohio. I had an enormous inferiority complex. I hated to go into a group of people. When I started to say something and wasn't saying it right, I would blush; and people would look at me and laugh. I hated to get up in the classroom to say anything because even when I thought I knew my facts, I was afraid I would make a fool of myself.[21]

On one occasion, after having been called upon to recite in class, the professor asked him to remain after class. As the other students departed, the professor said to Dr. Peale, "Why don't you stop thinking about yourself? Why do you think you freeze up the way you do when called on in class? Why do you get confused and tongue-tied and red in the face? Because you're stupid? No. Because you're lazy? No. It's because you're so full of you that there isn't room for anything else!" [22]

The professor had made his point. With new insight into his problem, Dr. Peale took a healthier view toward his studies. By the fall of his sophomore year, Dr. Peale's grades began to rise. Greek and required gym continued to be his downfall, but the rest of his grades were respectable by the end of that year. The state of his grades gradually improved until his final report in the spring of his senior year showed four "A's" and two "B's."

In the spring of his junior year, Dr. Peale was among those nominated for class president. Despite the fact that he lost, he ran fourth with a respectable sixty-three votes. It was during this time that he was particularly interested in a remark made by Professor "Rollie" Walker, who taught Bible. Professor Walker said: "Gentlemen, if you're interested in reaching large numbers of people, you'll do much better from behind an editor's desk than you will from a pulpit." [23] Dr. Peale knew that he possessed a certain verbal fluency, and he wondered also if his talents included the field of journalism. With his interest thus aroused, he became a staff member of the *Transcript,* the weekly student newspaper.

His interest in journalism was no passing fancy. He began to think seriously that a newspaper job might be the best stepping-stone to a political career, the vocation for which he was grooming himself. By his senior year, he was made editor of the *Transcript,* a recognized training ground for future journalists.

> At times he was sure that politics was his ultimate destiny, that a newspaper job would act as a springboard, and that once he took the plunge his gift for oratory would carry him far. He worked feverishly to improve this gift. He and another glib classmate, Oliver Jaynes, used to go out into a pasture at night, sit on the fence, and—fortified by a little elderberry wine— deliver impassioned orations, mostly on political themes. Then they would criticize each other's technique, pulling no punches.[24]

Before graduation day, Dr. Peale was to undergo one other

experience which bespeaks of his oratorical skill and organizational abilities. With the coming of the presidential election of 1920, the country was in a spirit of "buoyant optimism."

> In Ohio, Hiram Johnson, Warren Harding, and General Leonard Wood joined battle for the Republican nomination, and the excitement spread even to the cloistered halls of Ohio Wesleyan. One reason it spread was that Norman was busy spreading it. The manager of Wood's campaign conceived the idea that straw ballots on various campuses might be influential and useful—provided his candidate won them. He let it be known that funds might be available to any trustworthy undergraduate who would organize a "Win with Wood" campaign under the elms and capture the college vote.
>
> Down to Columbus went Norman with his friend and classmate "Joe" Joseph, both burning with newly acquired political fervor. They sought—and got—an interview with Wood's campaign manager. And they must have talked loud and long, because when they emerged from his office they were the official organizers of a "Win with Wood" campaign designed to sweep the campus back in Delaware. Even more astounding, they had been given the unheard-of sum of one hundred dollars with which to win friends and influence straw voters.[25]

Norman and Joe carried the "Win with Wood" campaign to a campus victory. Because of their efforts, they were invited to Columbus to sit on the platform with other notable guests to hear General Wood address a great rally. It was an experience to remember—something to talk about in future years. But now Norman had other things on his mind. He had arranged, upon graduation, to go to work for the *Findley Republican* as a cub reporter—salary, fifteen dollars per week.

The publisher of the *Findley Morning Republican*, Findley, Ohio, was Lowell Heminger; the city editor was Anson Hardman. Dr. Peale's first assignment was in a department where people are least likely to complain about treatment received at the hands of the press—obituaries. It was during this assignment that Dr. Peale saw the impact of death and sorrow on a household. It was his job to interview the survivors of the deceased, and when his father accompanied him, as he sometimes did, he saw the strength and hope that religion had to offer in such times of need. As he proved himself in obituaries, he progressed to covering police and fire activities.

After a few months' apprenticeship on the *Findley Morning Republican,* Dr. Peale was offered a job on the *Detroit Journal.* Grove Patterson, the editor, interviewed him and asked a few probing questions:

> "If you were writing for both a college professor and a ditch digger, to which one would you address your copy?" I was smart enough to answer that question. I replied that I would simplify my material so that the ditch digger could get it; then I would know that both readers could understand what I had written.[26]

Grove Patterson taught Dr. Peale a great deal about the techniques of reporting. Mr. Patterson was the newspaperman who said that the greatest literary device is a period. His philosophy about journalism was to keep all writing simple, uninvolved, and never obscure. "Use simple Anglo-Saxon words," he said, "and keep your sentences short." [27]

> "There's almost no subject," Patterson went on, "however complex, that can't be made understandable if the writer will just think clearly and write simply. There are precious few writers who can do this. Maybe you're one of 'em. I don't know. Let's try it for a while and see." [28]

In later life, Dr. Peale stated that he felt his newspaper experience offered valuable training for his career as a speaker. He commented:

> There's not a great deal of difference between writing a column and preparing a speech. The same basic advice applies: keep it simple, interesting, and brief.[29]

It did not take long, however, for Dr. Peale to realize that he did not possess the qualities needed in order to be a successful reporter. Looking at his fellow workers, he saw that they exhibited a certain toughness, aggressiveness, a ruthlessness, that he knew he did not have, nor want. The following incident crystallized this for him.

> He was sent with another reporter—a girl, as it happened—to the home of a man who had been involved in some sort of scandal and therefore was newsworthy. Their assignment was to interview the man's wife, and as they waited for her in the living room, Norman was already feeling squeamish about this intrusion on privacy. Suddenly the girl noticed on a table a photograph of the husband. She nudged Norman and pointed. "Slip that under your coat," she said. "What do you mean?" asked Norman startled. "I mean steal it," she said. "It's a good picture. No other paper will have it." When Norman still refused, she gave him a scornful look—and stole it herself.[30]

Still uncertain as to his vocational choice, Dr. Peale decided to enter Boston University to pursue a Master of Arts Degree in the graduate school and possibly take some courses in theology on the side.

Dr. Peale located himself in one of the oldest parts of the city of Boston—Louisburg Square. From the very first, he was fascinated by the city: "The sense of antiquity, of respect for and continuity with the past, the great religious traditions, the tacit

assumption of cultural superiority. . . ." [31] His four years at Ohio
Wesleyan had left much to be desired in the realm of classical
music and art. He compensated for these deficiences by going to
concerts and museums. Reading everything he could get his hands
on, "he discovered William James, and promptly elevated the
great psychologist to a pinnacle alongside Emerson in his pan-
theon of mighty American minds." [32]

Once again his area of interests shifted. He now planned to
work for two degrees: Bachelor of Sacred Theology and Master
of Arts in Social Ethics. In the spring of his first year at Boston, he
received word that the Methodist church in the little town of
Walpole, Massachusetts, had a pulpit to be filled on a particular
Sunday morning. Dr. Peale volunteered to accept the responsibility, though he had never before preached from a pulpit. For
two weeks he worked feverishly in the preparation of his sermon.
At least seven different versions of sermons built around his
father's favorite text ("I am come that they might have life, and
that they might have it more abundantly") were structured by his
painful efforts, but not one of them seemed to him worthy to
preach. Finally, as a last desperate hope, he wrote in panic to his
father, requesting some of his father's old notes—or a written
copy of one of his sermons. The reply came from his father in the
return mail. It said: "Prepare your own sermons. Just tell the
people that Jesus Christ can change their lives. Love—Dad." [33]

Dr. Peale's sermon in Walpole was only twelve minutes long.
Forgetting all about his prepared speech, he told simply in his
own words what Christ had done for him, and could do for them
if they would let Him. On the train back to Boston, he was overcome with the thought of a lifetime of sermons yet to prepare. He
was frightened by the fact that his first effort yielded only twelve
minutes. In twelve short minutes he had completely run dry; there
was nothing more for him to say. Then he realized that it was

ridiculous to think in terms of the thousands of sermons yet to be preached. An old saying came back to him: If the farmer thinks about all the corn he has to hoe, his back is broken before he starts! The way for him to handle the problem is to think about one thing at a time—and to accomplish it step by step.

Whenever possible, Dr. Peale spent the remainder of the year in the pulpit. The congregation from the church at Walpole invited him back on several occasions. Another little town in New Hampshire, Hancock, also invited him to fill the vacancy in their pulpit. These, however, were only temporary engagements.

In the summertime, after his first year at Boston University School of Theology, Dr. Peale returned to his home in Ohio. His father, by this time, had been appointed District Superintendent of an area covering perhaps a hundred churches. On the occasion of the illness of one of the ministers under his jurisdiction, he asked his son to step in and temporarily fill the vacancy.

Gladly he accepted his father's request, and set to work to produce a sermon that would do credit to the erudition of his teachers and the cultural spirit of old Boston. In an article published years later, Dr. Peale recalls this experience:

> I was imbued with everything that I was hearing in the classroom back at Boston School of Theology and at that particular time we were studying the atonement. Therefore, I prepared a ponderous, scholarly and intellectual sermon on the atonement, which I thought I would try out on the country folks that Sunday.
>
> I remember sitting on the front porch on Saturday afternoon, reading the sermon, from a manuscript, to my father. He sat with his feet perched on the porch rail, slumped back in the chair listening patiently and politely. When I had finished the manuscript, I asked him how he liked it.
>
> To this day I shall never forget his answer. He said, "Well, Norman, there are several things I would do with that sermon,

if I were you. First, I would go down in the cellar and put it in the furnace and burn it up. . . . Never preach from a manuscript. . . .

"It's a good thing to write it out so that you have good sentence structure and organize your thoughts, but having written it out, either put it away and don't use it, or burn it up. You must learn to get yourself so full of your message that you can stand before any group of people and pour it out to them, looking them directly in the eye while you do so."

Then he added another bit of advice. "The atonement is a great message, but you don't have to make it so involved. Scholarship isn't the use of obscure words or a language that is not plain. True scholarship," he said, "lets you take the greatest principles in the world and make them so simple that a child can understand them. Did not the greatest teacher of all, Jesus, do that by the simple illustrations he used?

"So," he told me, "you go out and tell the people that Jesus Christ died for them; that He died to save them from sin and from confusion and from fear and from hate. Just tell them in simple everyday American farm language; words of one, or two, or three syllables; strong, sturdy, American words, that Jesus Christ can save them from themselves and give them joy and peace, and make their lives fruitful in the field of service. Go out and talk to the people about the atoning grace of Jesus Christ in a language they'll understand. Make it short, make it interesting, and above all tell them what you personally know. Do not try to give them theoretical religion. Give them a statement of your personal experience of Jesus Christ." [34]

Dr. Peale went on to say that when time came for the sermon, he heeded his father's advice and gave a simple sermon based entirely on his own spiritual experience. "Again, the sermon was short because it didn't take me long to tell the little I knew." [35] At the conclusion of the sermon, one of the country parishioners approached him with the following advice:

"You did all right this morning, Son. Your sermon was simple and everybody could understand it." He chuckled, "Even I could understand it. There wasn't a big word in it. Never put any big words in your sermons," he said, "because you must not act proud, smug, or try to impress people. Remember you should always talk to the knowledge of the least educated person in your congregation." [36]

The random advice which he had been receiving made an impact on Dr. Peale's thinking. It was during his second year at Divinity school that he made a conscious effort to analyze and understand the techniques of the successful preacher. He knew that outstanding preachers were few and far between. "Listening to his elders and betters, watching them conduct themselves in the pulpit or on the lecture platform, Dr. Peale began to ask himself seriously and earnestly what it was that made some good and some indifferent." [37] Using his own personal reaction and the observable reactions of the audiences as a standard of judgment, he analyzed what it was that the successful speaker possessed.

> They were *arresting:* they caught the audience's attention at the start with some striking statement or anecdote, and then they held it. They were *logical:* their ideas were presented in a sequence that led the listener eventually to the point they were trying to make. They had *personality:* humor, enthusiasm, dedication, sincerity, a quality of differentness. Almost always they were *simple,* clear, unpretentious—and brief.
>
> And where the great preachers were concerned, there was one more quality that was the most important of all: the mysterious and incandescent impressions that they projected of *being used,* of being a transmission mechanism for a mighty flow of truth and power that came from beyond them and passed through them into the minds and hearts of man.[38]

Poor preachers were also found, by Dr. Peale, to have certain characteristics in common:

They had little knowledge of what really appealed to people —and consequently rarely made any appeal to people's interest in their own betterment. They were unable to think clearly for any sustained length of time—and so were unable to offer any logical progression of ideas. They distrusted simplicity for fear that they themselves would be thought unlearned—and consequently added pedantry to obscurity. They almost never used the God-given faculty of humor—either because they had little to begin with or because they had somehow come to believe it was out of place in the pulpit.

They had a tendency to talk too long because, having no empathy with their audience, they were unaware of the degree of boredom they were generating. They had been taught to preach mainly about great social evils rather than immediate problems of their parishioners, so they chose broad topics—and the broader the topic, the less the impact on the individual. Finally, a great many of them had adopted a hollowness of tone, a kind of empty ecclesiastical sonority that was both sanctimonious and soporific. They were dealing with the most thrilling, fascinating thing in the world, the Gospel of Jesus Christ, and they were making it sound dull.[39]

In the spring of the second year in Boston, Dr. Peale was given an opportunity to show what he could do on a more permanent basis. He was appointed minister of the Methodist church in the town of Berkeley, Rhode Island. Berkeley lay in the rugged Blackstone Valley, halfway between Pawtucket and Woonsocket.

It offered little in the way of charm or natural beauty; just a handful of homes clinging to the rocky hillsides and the grim brick rectangles that were the mills. The church, a tiny frame structure, was perched precariously just above the main road.[40]

Such an opportunity as this provided excellent training for a seminary student. When a question of policy or problem of im-

portance arose concerning the church, the young and inexperi-
enced minister could carry it back to the divinity school and dis-
cuss it with older and wiser men. Similarly, the new material
acquired in seminary could be immediately put to the test of a
real life situation. Dr. Peale benefited greatly from this "laboratory" experience. However, the experience was had without the
benefit of any prior courses in speech, for none was available to
seminary students. Dr. Peale feels this was most unfortunate. "I
have always regretted that I didn't have the opportunity to take
a course in public speaking. I had to learn by trial and error—a
process which was, I fear, rather hard on my congregations." [41]

Though no speech courses were available, Dr. Peale felt that
one of his professors in seminary, Professor George S. Butters,
offered some valuable suggestions concerning speech and sermon-
making.

> He urged us to talk to our congregations about what they
> were interested in, and to make our sermons simple. He also
> told us that in order to preach effectively we had, as he put it,
> to "get in there and love the congregation." I early found how
> practical this advice was. I'll never forget one humorous but
> excellent piece of advice he gave. Professor Butters was a prac-
> tical person as well as a great soul. "Men," he said, "no matter
> how carefully you have prepared your sermons, sometimes
> you're going to get stuck. When that happens, just trust in the
> Lord and keep the blessed sound agoing." [42]

When Dr. Peale's seminary years came to a close, armed with
a Master's Degree in Social Ethics and a Bachelor's Degree in
Sacred Theology, he was appointed minister of the Flatlands
Church in Brooklyn, New York. The ceremony was held in the
month of May, in the year 1924. Officially, he was made associate
minister of St. Marks Methodist Church at Ocean Avenue and
Beverly Road, an older and stronger congregation that generously
sponsored the struggling little church of forty members.

Not merely content to call on prospective members, Dr. Peale kept in contact with his constituents by constantly bombarding them with postcards, letters, and leaflets. He was out to sell Christianity, and his church in particular.

> Sometimes the cards would ask provocative questions. "Why have our congregations increased until the church is crowded to capacity? Why has Sunday school attendance increased 100% in six months? Why are unchurched people of every Protestant denomination coming to us in increasingly large numbers? Come around and your questions will be answered."
>
> Sometimes the postcards would reach unashamedly for an emotional effect. "Do you remember," they would ask nostalgically, "the hymns your mother used to sing? You can hear them again, you know!" Or, "Palm Sunday—what memories it brings! The warm sunshine of spring, robin redbreasts on the lawn, the unfolding flowers. Visions of Mother getting the family ready, then the crowded church, the stately old hymns, a great congregation lifting their voices in the triumphant chorus! You, too, can be a part of this. Come next Sunday!" [43]

At the end of six months crowds were so large that the church building had to be abandoned, services being held in a large tent set up on the lot where the New Flatlands Church was to be built. The lot was on the corner of Kings Highway and East 37th Street, and on September 20, 1925, the new Kings Highway Church was dedicated. By 1926 the membership in the Kings Highway Church had risen to 900, the Sunday School was the largest in Brooklyn, and Dr. Peale was now an experienced minister.

In his twenty-eighth year, Dr. Peale was called as minister to the University Methodist Church in Syracuse, New York. He officially began his pastorate there on May 22, 1927. Though the atmosphere was entirely different from the Brooklyn church, the problems were the same. Of the six thousand students at Syracuse University, only a handful attended Sunday services. The empty seats in the church each Sunday bespoke of the religious sterility of its members.

The man who welcomed Dr. Peale to Syracuse, and who introduced him to the congregation, was destined to become one of his best friends—Hugh M. Tilroe, Dean of the College of Public Speaking at Syracuse University.

Dr. Peale's first weeks were filled with tension and anxiety. "I knew I was in a university pulpit and therefore I thought I had to preach very scholarly sermons. I attempted to do that. I read heavy books and quoted learned authority. In fact I tried to preach a baccalaureate sermon every Sunday morning." [44] In his car Dr. Peale carried the Oxford Book of English Verse, and he quoted frequently from Carlyle, Victor Hugo, Addison, Jung, Dostoievsky, Marcus Aurelius, Plato, and others. Needless to say, the congregation was amazed and somewhat appalled. Finally, in an effort to get Dr. Peale back on the right track, Dean Bray, one of the most learned members of the faculty, asked him out for lunch. In a friendly and helpful way Dean Bray said:

> I would like to make a little suggestion. You think that we, being college professors, want an intellectualized sermon. Now . . . you must remember something about us. We may be experts in our fields; one man in biology, another in geology, another in history. Each man is presumably an expert in the field of his studies. You must be an expert in the field of *spirit*. You must realize, when we come down to listen to you on Sunday, that we look up to you as the teacher, and you must tell us what you, personally, know about this, not what somebody said about it in a book that you are going to quote. . . .
>
> And remember this . . . , we are all men and women who need God. We're just poor sinful people and you mustn't be so awed by us that you cannot tell us directly wherein we are wrong and need repentance. Preach to us the same as you would to anybody else.[45]

Dean Tilroe said much the same thing to Dr. Peale. He was a huge man, a man's man as Dr. Peale would refer to him, who had a cabin on a lake back in the woods where he loved to fish and hunt. The cabin had two bunks, and Dr. Peale spent many a week-end with him, revealing his innermost thoughts and establishing a lasting friendship.

This bit of information passed on by Deans Tilroe and Bray was the medicine Dr. Peale needed. He realized that he had been too sedate, too cautious in his approach. So once again he turned to the techniques which had been so successful in Brooklyn. He placed advertisements in the Syracuse *Post-Standard:* "Why are young people flocking to the University Church? Why is it suddenly hard to get a seat?" This was the way he visualized it, and so to him it had already become a fact.

On the campus of the university, just six blocks away, were 6000 boys and girls.

> I conceived the idea of having a different fraternity come every Sunday. I roped off a section with fraternity colors, and had them even send notices to all their alumni to invite them to come and occupy a reserved section. They began to vie with one another to have the largest turnout.[46]

In addition, he assembled the best singers he could find under the direction of Dr. Howard Lyman of the University's Music Department and called the result "the greatest choir in the Empire State!" He revived and revised his postcard mailing list. Having seen an appropriate motto on a hotel menu, he adopted it for his church: "Where you're a stranger but once . . ." He had professionals from New York come up and give readings of plays and dramatizations of Bible stories.

No doubt some of Dr. Peale's showmanship attracted people to his church. But he did not feel it was showmanship that held them, that kept them coming back. It was the message, old to some, new to others, that Christianity worked:

> All I wanted was to get them there to preach the Gospel to them. The Gospel itself was attractive: it wasn't the way I put it up that made it attractive; it wasn't that I was an orator, for I never have been an orator or even in any sense an eloquent speaker. But I have always tried to tell people about Jesus.[47]

Because of Dr. Peale's new enthusiasm and leadership, the church grew in size. His interests grew with the church, and soon he had a radio program, *The Angelus Hour,* which brought him into contact with a greatly expanded audience every Saturday afternoon. He drove himself endlessly. Working from dawn to the early hours of the following morning, planning and improving his speeches, sermons, and radio talks. There was also poetry to be memorized, quotations to be filed away, and always the endless details of church administration. In addition, a lecture bureau offered to take him under its wing:

> . . . the percentage it demanded from its clients was absurdly high. But Norman didn't care. He was impressed by the brochure that introduced him—with more enthusiasm than knowledge of French—as "The Beaux Ideal of Youth." "Culture and elegance," cried the leaflet, "walk right into your community with Peale!" Then, under the heading "Peale's Appeal," it went on to give synopses of various orations. "Poetry, philosophy, literature and all the sciences, in an amazing roll call are called upon to testify to the worth of personality." [48]

In appreciation of his loyalty to the faculty and students of Syracuse University, Syracuse University conferred on him the honorary degree of Doctor of Divinity in the spring of 1931.

By now Dr. Peale was sought after by other large churches. He declined an invitation to fill the pulpit of the largest Methodist congregation in Indiana—the Methodist Church in Indianapolis. He delivered in 1932, however, a guest sermon at Marble Collegiate Church in New York City and was thereafter invited to take over the dwindling congregation. He accepted and thus obtained the leadership of the oldest chartered church in New York (1696).

> The word "Collegiate" stood for the ministry of Colleagues in Marble, Middle, West End, Fort Washington, and St. Nicholas congregations. These congregations together comprised the Collegiate Church in America, popularly known as the Dutch Reformed Church.
>
> Its history dated from 1628 when the Dutch established it in Nieuw Amsterdam. The church had served under three flags, Dutch, British, and American, and was the oldest institution of any kind in New York. The first colonial governor, Peter Stuyvesant, was a member, as was Peter Minuit, who purchased the Island of Manhattan from the Indians for twenty-four dollars.[49]

When Dr. Peale arrived, Marble Collegiate Church had been without a minister for three years. In the meantime, under a succession of temporary pastors, the congregation had dwindled. Only two hundred people were attending the Sunday services in the nave designed to seat eight times that many. The nation was experiencing a dismal year—the low point of the depression. People were tense, uneasy, and unhappy. Men were jumping out of windows, having nervous breakdowns and heart attacks. People were frightened, discouraged, and in many cases utterly defeated. The suicide rate had rapidly increased. Many people had lost faith in past creeds which no longer seemed applicable to the practical human problems of the world.

Dr. Peale began with as much enthusiasm as in his past pastorates, but the results were slow in materializing. He preached three sermons a week: Sunday morning, Sunday evening, and Wednesday evening. Yet, in 1934, after two years of hard work, the church still showed little evidence of its once religious vitality. But the experience was beneficial because Dr. Peale realized he could no longer preach as academic a sermon as he did at Syracuse.

> The very times compelled me to address myself to human needs; telling brokenhearted, frustrated people that there was healing and renewal in the simple principles which Jesus taught.[50]
>
> I knew that they didn't want to hear abstract theological dialection; they wanted immediate help with the problems they had to face every day. So I launched into a concentrated study of psychology. Gradually I evolved what might be considered a scientific approach to meet the needs of a modern society.[51]

Taking his texts from both the Old and New Testaments, Dr. Peale interpreted Christianity as a highly useful scientific and modern commodity for modern people, and he dispensed it with the same kind of skill that a salesman used in selling shoes, stoves, or automobiles.

He was deeply impressed by the way a psychiatrist, given the salient facts, could penetrate the carefully erected defenses of a patient, brush aside the camouflage, and reach the heart of the problem. Speaking of this ability of the psychiatrist, he said:

> It's simply amazing . . . to watch him analyze a situation, probe into a maladjusted personality, find the basic reason why a man can't get along with his wife, or keeps failing in his work, or suffers from hypertension. Once the psychiatrist points out the basic cause, then we ministers can begin to apply the great remedies of religion: prayer, faith, and love. But the two therapies go together . . . They complement each other.[52]

Through the initiative of Dr. Peale and Dr. Smiley Blanton, a Religio-Psychiatric Clinic was developed in the Church. At first

Drs. Blanton and Peale were the sole staff members, but the Clinic grew until presently it is the American Foundation for Religion and Psychiatry and has a staff of professional counselors, psychiatrists, psychologists, and ministerial training candidates. Dr. Peale uses the Clinic "to clinch the nail he drives in with his sermons on Sunday." [53] He feels that psychiatry has to do with the upsets of the mind, heart, and soul. It deals with mental and spiritual tensions, frustrations, and confusions. Dr. Peale looks on it as a science made to order for the preacher. He readily admits that he likes to employ psychology in his sermons. He finds it an aid to reaching the needs of his listeners.

> He lays no claim to being a psychiatrist himself: he is a preacher, a minister, a counselor in the things of the spirit, and no more. That's why, when he organized the Clinic, he went to Dr. Smiley Blanton, one of the recognized psychiatrists of New York City, and asked him to become a partner in the enterprise. He sold Dr. Blanton on the idea that a minister and psychiatrist, working together, could lift the living and restore the faith of countless people who were plagued by pestilences in the darkness. The partnership became a fact; it works beautifully. Today twelve other psychiatrists and psychologists, and a social psychiatrist assist Doctors Peale and Blanton on the Staff. [54]

Thus, within a relatively short time after his arrival at Marble Collegiate Church, Dr. Peale realized that if a minister was to be versed in the problems of modern man, he must understand and make use of the modern behavioral sciences. The truths of the Bible were the same, but their interpretation had to be adjusted to meet the needs of modern man.

A second philosophy of Dr. Peale's began to take root shortly after his arrival in New York City. From early childhood, Dr. Peale had been asking himself why the women far outnumber the men in any given congregation. ". . . I noticed that increasingly

the church was losing its hold upon men, at least from the stand-
point of active participation in its work and from a profound influence of the Gospel in their daily lives and inner experiences." [55]

One night in New York he attended and spoke at a very large
gathering of men; the average age in the group being somewhere
in the late thirties or early forties. He viewed them as being "outstanding, alert, vigorous, dynamic business and professional men."
But upon inquiry, he found that it was a general consensus that
only a minor percentage of these men were actively interested in
church life.

> It came over me then with a tremendous surge of importance
> that we needed to recruit the vast and amazing manpower avail-
> able to the Christian church.
>
> I had a definite spiritual experience that night, . . . I told
> the Lord that if He would guide me, I would do everything in
> my power to bring about a great resurgence of dedication
> among the men of America to Christ and the Church. [56]

"Under God's guidance, I was soon offered an opportunity to
lecture under lecture bureau auspices before business and industrial conventions." [57] Before long, the most time-consuming of all
his activities was his ever-increasing lecture program. Starting at
$10 to $25 each lecture, his salary quickly advanced to from $400
to $600 per lecture. His lecture activities carried him throughout
the United States, and by 1953 he was speaking some eighty-five
or ninety times a winter to audiences of all kinds and sizes.

> On a Tuesday he might address a bankers' convention in
> Tulsa. On Thursday he might speak to 50,000 people assembled
> in the Cotton Bowl at Dallas. On Friday night it might be a
> National Realtors' Meeting in Chicago. He might cross the
> country from east to west, or from north to south, but always,
> like a sort of spiritual homing pigeon, he had to be back in his
> Fifth Avenue pulpit on Sunday morning. [58]

In his travels and speeches at business and industrial conventions, Dr. Peale found that men wanted something said about how to meet the stress and strain of their lives. One night when he was scheduled to speak at a large convention, a young businessman was introduced to him. "Tell me, Dr. Peale," the man said, "exactly what is your formula for living?" Dr. Peale replied, "Well, I suppose it's twofold: to find the secret of effective living for one's self, and then, having done so, to try to help others find their answer." He went on to explain that he had found that secret in religion—in the Gospel of Jesus Christ.

> "If that's true," said the man, "why aren't more of us businessmen aware of it and interested in it?" He hesitated, then answered his own question. "I'll tell you why. Because nobody tells us about it in language we can understand. We've quit going to church, most of us, because we've come to associate churches with boredom. And the church never comes to us. Why don't you fellows come down out of the pulpit once in a while and talk to us on our own level and in our own language at meetings like this one, or at business conventions? Outside the church, anyway! The message would be just as valid, wouldn't it? Why don't you go out and buttonhole us wherever we are? If what you have to offer is worth having, we'll listen. And maybe after a while we'll start going to church. But first you've got to play the game on our home grounds, not yours. If you want us in your churches, some of you have got to get out on the road and sell your product! You've got to be missionaries to businessmen!" [59]

Dr. Peale took such advice to heart. He attempted to formulate his sermons as well as his lectures so as to appeal to the American businessman. The secret, he felt, was to appeal to their needs; then, they would respond. Their needs centered around the problems of facing fear, anxiety, frustration, failure, depression, self-consciousness, lack of enthusiasm, etc.

Thus, to Dr. Peale, analyzing his audience has become a consideration of vast importance. He feels that the audience— whether it be a Sunday congregation or a weekday business convention—has a "corporate personality" of its own. "It could be alive, intent, aware of everything. It could also be apathetic, lethargic, dull; but it could be influenced, it could be coaxed, it could be challenged—and it would almost always respond." [60] Dr. Peale further feels that "to be persuasive, a preacher or any public speaker must have a keen understanding of human psychology; he must have a sympathetic understanding of the wants and desires of his listeners." [61] And he must shape his message to meet the needs as he sees them. It is through such an analysis that the minister is able to sense the mood or atmosphere of his audience. This is an essential part of successful preaching.

> One of the queerest phenomena in a speaker's world is this thing called mood or atmosphere. I never quite understand it. You give the same speech to the same kind of people. They wear the same kind of clothes, the same kind of ties, the same kind of collars. The speech is the same; you are the same person making it. But the mood in one place is more receptive, more electric than in others.[62]

Having analyzed the audience, the next step in preparing a lecture or sermon is to find an appropriate topic. In an interview with Eugene White, presently at Pennsylvania State University, and Clair Henderlider of Western Reserve University, for the *Quarterly Journal of Speech*, Dr. Peale gave the following views on sermonizing.

The topic should always be one which can be framed in a "concise, definite statement, such as: 'How to stop being tense,' or 'How to lose fear through faith!' " [63] Since the minister should be concerned with the needs of his audience, the problem-solving sermon is the most important tool he has.

The sermon itself should be outlined under two basic headings. Roman numeral I represents the introduction, and II the main body of the speech.

The introduction has several purposes. One purpose is to stimulate interest and attention.

> An excellent way of getting attention is to point out the importance of the topic. In a recent sermon, I began like this: "One of the most important of human problems is what to do about one's failures. You can use a failure to go on to successful living; or you can permit a failure to destroy you." Sometimes I start off with a question or two. I might say: "Do you know how to make things turn out right? How many times have you heard a person complain, 'Why does everything go wrong for me?' " I also make frequent use of quotations, examples, and snatches of dialogue.[64]

Another purpose of the introduction is to provide the minister a place to state his thesis.

> For example, in a sermon, *Peace for the Troubled Mind,* my opening sentence was, "The purpose of this talk is to help people discover the secret of peace for the troubled mind." In another sermon, *Lose Your Fears Through Faith,* I began with, "Would you like to lose your fears? Well, you can. The way to do it is through Faith." [65]

The introduction to lectures or occasional speeches should be essentially the same as those of sermons. In addition, however, they provide an excellent opportunity to make some personal reference to the situation, the audience, or to the purpose of the meeting. This technique is a great aid to developing the interest and attention factors.

There should not be more than three main subheads under the body of the speech—Roman numeral II in Dr. Peale's outline. If it is possible to cover the material under two headings, then that is so much the better. The more major points the minister presents, the more complex the speech becomes, and the more confusion that will develop in the minds of the listeners.

> My sermons and speeches are essentially problem-solving. Usually I present the problem quickly under "I," the introduction . . . this allows me to utilize "II" in answering the problem. Usually the two or three subheads under "II" represent specific guides, or methods for solving the problem.[66]

It is not necessary to provide a separate section in the outline for the conclusion. "What I do is to summarize after each subhead under 'II.' Therefore, the summary for the last heading serves as a conclusion for the entire speech." [67] Concluding remarks should be short and to the point.

The minister should follow his outline carefully. He should never use spur-of-the-moment material—only that which has been carefully thought out and evaluated beforehand. A sermon should be about twenty-five minutes in length; and if the minister finds that he is running out of time, he can omit the last capital letter heading under Roman numeral II. Since a summary is given after each subheading, the summary after B would serve as well for the close of the entire sermon as would the summary for the heading C.

In regard to delivery, Dr. Peale states that the minister should speak extemporaneously whenever possible. He should carefully prepare a pattern or sequence of ideas and leave the exact expression of those ideas to the inspiration of the moment. The reading or memorizing of a sermon injures spontaneity. Without spontaneity there can be little rapport between the speaker and his audience.

Dr. Peale states that he "picturizes" the outline of his sermon rather than "memorizes" it.

> Usually when someone speaks of memorizing an outline, he means that he learns verbatim the precise wording. What I do

is to "picturize" in my mind the sequence and the relationships of the major and minor points. By following this procedure and by memorizing all quotations and statistics, I avoid using notes during delivery.[68]

If a minister has a definite mannerism of voice or gesture which he wishes to correct, it would be good to practice in front of a mirror or before a friend. It is not necessary under ordinary circumstances to practice a sermon by reciting it. It is a good practice, however, to go over the sermon a number of times in one's mind.

It is not necessary to use particular gestures or inflections at certain places in the sermon. It is sufficient merely to depend upon one's body and voice to respond appropriately to the situation. The minister should present his message in a simple, interesting, and forceful manner. The delivery should be animated, vital, and positive, and the voice should be in a style as close to conversation as fits the occasion. Special emphasis should be given to not being spectacular, artificial, or overly emotional.

Dr. Peale feels that spiritual mobilization is just as important as mechanical preparation, and for that reason the minister should never enter a pulpit—or platform—without experiencing, through prayer, the power of Divine guidance. Preaching is not something to enter into without having first looked to God for help and guidance. In order to "condition" himself before facing an audience, Dr. Peale always tries to have some time for meditation, "during which I go over my speech carefully and pray for Divine assistance." His conviction that God will assist him during his speech is one of the important sources of his poise and confidence as a speaker. ". . . I believe that I am merely the agent of God's will and that He will give me effective expression." [69] In other words, the minister must have a sense of "being used" by God. A ministry that is self-appointed on the basis of the recognition of need on the one hand and of special gifts on the other might do well enough, from the human point of view, if there could be an assurance of fair weather for the entire voyage. But the course of this ministry does not run through such a calm sea.

Among contemporary theologians and ministers, Dr. Peale was soon recognized for his belief that doctrine and dogma should be minimized and Christianity made a practical, usable faith for a modern world. The message developed by Dr. Peale brought the businessmen into his church and gave him the title, the "Businessmen's Preacher." Today, more than 60% of his congregation are men, for they especially seem to respond to his simple, direct approach to God.

Dr. Peale worked hard to meet the challenge of the New York metropolitan area referred to as "the graveyard of ministers." Little by little his congregation rose in numbers. Besides preaching to the needs of the businessman, he hammered away at social themes. He recognized the peril that shadows all ministers from the first day of their ministry to the last day. This peril is the temptation to become suave and genial to the point of losing all dependable effectiveness. The nature of the minister's work makes this tendency inevitable. If he is really to minister to people he must live with them, speak their language, and gain their confidence. This means that he must cultivate the qualities in his life which make him agreeable and likable. A major part of all his associations pull him in the direction of things that are peaceful and consoling. If he is not careful, a little yielding here and a slight compromise there will soon make him a man who is harmless and, ultimately, ineffective.

It is for this reason that Dr. Peale never regretted having had the experience of a newspaper reporter—for he felt it an advantageous training ground for his later work in the ministry. Not only did he improve his writing skills as a newspaper reporter, but many of the techniques he learned were employed in the construction of his sermons later on. In addition, the experience provided him with a background of the struggles and sorrows and failures and yearnings of ordinary, harassed, bedeviled human beings—people groping for happiness and the chance to become better than they knew themselves to be. This is important, for above all else Dr. Peale felt that the minister must be down to earth. A cloud dweller in the ministry would never be a success in meeting the needs of his people.

> Ministers should have knowledge of human beings; they should be aware of the tough, cheap, and tawdry side of existence. One cannot know these things if he lives a cloistered life. In the city room of a newspaper office, I was taught to see the truth and have the courage to deal with the facts. If you think about it . . . you'll realize that is the job of a minister, too.[70]

If a minister is to be worth his salt, then, he must know not only the still waters and the quiet places but also the enemies both within the fold and on the outside that are harmful to Christian teachings. However strongly inclined he may be toward the ways of peace, he knows that the element of conflict is in all of life, and he must not back down in the face of sin. Without losing the sympathetic touch which enables him to bring comfort where it is needed, the minister must develop a toughness of fiber that does not yield to the threats of arrogant and entrenched evil. In other words, "if you can find a good fight, you had better get into it." But be certain that it is a "good fight."

Like many other ministers, Dr. Peale went through the experience of engaging himself and his congregation in needless controversy because he had not been able to distinguish between a real principle and marginal custom. Throughout the Second World War, and for a few years thereafter, he clung to the belief that a minister had not only the right but the duty to speak out on political affairs, presidential elections, social issues, etc. In the middle 1930's his views on drinking brought him into controversy with Mrs. Eleanor Roosevelt. She was quoted as saying that "intelligent young ladies ought to find out what their capacity for drinking was, and then stay within it." Dr. Peale, President of the American Temperance Society, was so stunned by her views—and particularly by the fact that a person in her position would condone drinking at all—that he reprimanded her vehemently from the pulpit. The New York newspapers saw "increased sales" in the controversy and played it up to such an extent that Dr. Peale and Mrs. Roosevelt were finally convinced by a mutual friend that they should meet and try to still the troubled waters. The meeting, however, was not a success, for the tolerance expressed in a statement prepared by Mrs. Roosevelt was still not in keeping with Dr. Peale's conservative views.

In 1948 Dr. Peale favored the nomination of General Mac-Arthur on the Republican ticket. Later he supported his neighbor, Governor Thomas Dewey, in his campaign against Truman. Slowly but surely, however, he became aware of the factions that develop in a church when the minister takes stands on issues outside the realm of pure theology. Partisan activities on the part of a minister are divisive; they alienate people. They reduce the effectiveness of the pastor as spiritual leader of a united congregation. It was this conclusion that led Dr. Peale to make the following statement:

> I've been wrong . . . I've done my ministry a lot of harm by getting mixed up in political activities . . . I'm through with this sort of organization. I've got my spiritual work, and I'm going to stick to that. Believe me, from this point on, if the country were collapsing, and a committee were formed to save the Republic, I wouldn't join it! [71]

Later, disregarding this statement, Dr. Peale came to realize that there are issues today that are related to human welfare, personal and national decency, and international relations about which the Church cannot compromise without forfeiting its right to speak for God. The minister must decide for himself the merits of the issue, then act accordingly.

During the 1960 campaign for President of the United States, Dr. Peale attended a meeting in Washington, D. C., titled the "National Conference of Citizens for Religious Freedom." [72]

This group adopted a declaration which, in essence, expressed concern for future church-state relationships. The group was not representative of all Protestants, however, and reaction came quickly from more liberal Protestants who violently disagreed. Reinhold Niebuhr, James A. Pike, Paul Tillich, and John C. Bennett were quick to denounce Dr. Peale, who, while not in any sense the leader of this meeting, took the brunt of the criticism. Editorials favoring and denouncing Dr. Peale's stand quickly spread throughout the country.

As a result of the entire incident, Dr. Peale offered to resign his pulpit at Marble Collegiate Church. His congregation felt differently, however, and gave him a "standing tribute." His wife said that, in his 29 years at the Church, this marked the first time he had received such a tribute.

Dr. Peale felt that he did not do anything wrong, just unwise. He said he probably would not have attended the meeting in the first place if he had not planned to be in Washington to attend a day-long religious retreat the following day.

> I felt a sense of concern about the matter of religious free-
> dom and believe it is proper at any time for a Protestant to
> meet with fellow Protestants to discuss matters relating to our
> faith.

He went on to say:

> It is the American right to assemble and to consider, and in
> this instance it was done with dignity and with a view towards

lifting the religious discussion towards a higher intellectual level and to divest it of heat and emotionalism.

I might have known, and I am amazed that I did not realize that under the circumstances this would immediately get involved in the political campaign. I sincerely did not mean it to be so, but perhaps I will be a wiser person in the future—at least, let us hope so.

. . . I do not feel that I was wrong in attending this meeting, but it may have been unwise under the circumstances.

Despite such occasional incidents, the Marble Collegiate Church, under Dr. Peale's guidance, continued to increase its membership. And with the increase in membership came also an increase in responsibility for Dr. Peale. This, however, was exactly what Dr. Peale wanted. He had little patience with those who deplored bigness in religion. He felt that numbers do count. If the world was to be won for Christianity, the people of the world must be reached.

We ministers are sometimes accused of being too concerned with full pews. I plead guilty. I freely subscribe to the notion that we must capture the world with Christianity, not just rescue a small remnant.[73]

Dr. Peale feels that, in an effort to reach as large an audience as possible, it is the minister's duty to make use of all available means of mass communication. He, himself, had no doubt that Saint Paul would have gladly used television if it had been available to him. Consequently, his interests embraced every field in the area of communications. In order to spread his Christian message, he makes extensive use of radio, television, syndicated newspaper articles, magazine articles, books, pamphlets, and advertising brochures of all shapes and sizes. At the proposal of a friend, he even wrote brief messages for Easter and Christmas cards—

and was paid accordingly. His feeling is that these man-made avenues for communication can just as well be made to serve God's purpose as any other purpose.

By 1955, Dr. Peale's book, *The Power of Positive Thinking,* had taken the world like wildfire. Over two million copies had been sold. In addition, 4000 people heard him preach in person each Sunday. An overflow crowd of worshipers saw and heard him on closed-circuit television in the basement of the Marble Collegiate Church. His weekly syndicated column "Confident Living" was being carried in over 100 newspapers. It was estimated that his radio talks, *The Art of Living,* entered 1,000,000 homes each week. A television show which he shared with his wife, *What's Your Trouble,* was carried by over 100 stations. He was editor of an inspirational monthly bulletin called *Guideposts,* with a circulation of 625,000 and over 300,000 followers received his weekly sermons through the mail. In addition to these endeavors, he helped run, free of charge, a religio-psychiatric clinic which annually counseled over 1000 cases. Self-help cards were written and distributed to anyone desiring them, and long-playing records of his sermons were available to the public.

The name, Dr. Norman Vincent Peale, was literally known by millions of people throughout the world. As a man of great influence, and as a renowned speaker, Dr. Peale had "arrived." He had not become the politician which was his great dream as a college student—but he had become perhaps the most popular minister in the world.

Chapter 3

The Public Image

For Dr. Peale the road to the national limelight has not been one of total glory. Like all other leaders, he has made enemies as well as friends. For purposes of analyzing Dr. Peale's public image, this chapter will be divided into two sections: (A) The Case Against Dr. Peale, and (B) The Case in Favor of Dr. Peale.

THE CASE AGAINST DR. PEALE

From newspaper and magazine articles, one might quickly conclude that Dr. Peale's antagonists are composed mostly of members of his own profession. However, the preaching of Dr. Norman Vincent Peale and other Protestant ministers with a similar approach has come under sharp criticism and attack by both laymen and clergymen; some of the religious objections come from such high theological sources that they cannot be dismissed lightly as the products of personal envy or professional jealousy. The complaints of these critics range from mild assertions that Dr. Peale's optimistic interpretation of the Gospel is repetitious and oversimplified to the grave charge that what he is preaching is not Christianity at all, but represents an attempt to manipulate God in accordance with the selfish and materialistic desires of sinful man. The chief accusation is that by his emphasis on the power of faith and "positive thinking," Dr. Peale is diminishing in his audience the consciousness of inborn sin and of moral help-lessness without the grace of God that are traditional and (the theologians agree) essential Christian doctrines. Dr. Peale, accord-ing to these critics, is teaching only half-truths; he is preaching partial Christianity.

It is difficult to put an exact label on this newly popularized re-ligious trend, for critics refer to it in their own descriptive terms. But consensus among the critics can be found in such phrases as "easy religion," "positive thinking," and "the cult of reassurance." For the last decade ministers throughout the country have been speaking from their pulpits against the idea that Christianity is "simply a way to get selfish peace of mind or a shield for one's own life." An example of the extent to which this topic is being discussed and studied in religious circles was the report at the general assembly of Southern Presbyterians in June of 1955. This report condemned the use of religious faith "to manipulate God and bring Him to do our will." [74]

The new "cult of reassurance" is reminiscent of the technique of "conscious auto-suggestion" which was popularized just after the First World War by Dr. Emile Coué. His formula for better living was to repeat twenty times each morning, "Every day in every way I am getting better and better."

Some of the critics of the new religion of reassurance have pointed out that its recent emergence probably dates from 1946 when the best-selling book *Peace of Mind,* by Rabbi Liebman, was published. The success of this book, which attempted to show how religious faith and psychology could be combined to reduce the tensions of modern life, brought many imitators. Lay hold of the master key to the life within you, Marcus Bach recommends in a recently published book, and you can acquire *The Will to Believe.* Just learn to think well of yourself, Dr. Hyman Schachtel urges, and you will get *The Life You Want To Live.* You can achieve spiritual sovereignty, Dr. Roy Burkhart assures, by acquiring *The Freedom to Become Yourself*. Harness *The Magic Power of Your Mind*, Walter Germain encourages, and you can live twenty-four hours a day. Learn to pray while at work, George Murron insists, and you will find that *There Is a Place for God in Business*. Forget the "ifs" in your life and you will discover, according to Alexander Lake, that *Your Prayers Are Always Answered*.

The "peace of mind" message has been spread not only by clergymen who preach it in books and articles but those who utilize it in their sermons and personal counseling. Although other ministers use the same approach, Dr. Peale's name seems to predominate when this subject is under discussion in religious circles. In the past few years, he has become perhaps America's best-known Protestant preacher. Perhaps it is because of this great popularity that Paul Hutchinson, editor of *The Christian Century*, leading undenominational Protestant publication, has labeled Dr. Peale "the high priest of this cult of reassurance." [75]

To summarize the views of the critics, it is not the "man" but the "message" that they are attacking. They are concerned over the fact that millions of people are accepting a "quasi-Christianity," a Christianity designed to mislead, distort, and confuse. The critics feel that this new era of religion, this new faith, has little to do with the old-fashioned faith as Saint Paul conceived it —the faith of the contrite Christian humbly imploring the mercy and guidance of the Almighty to fight off sin and temptation. That is a negative approach to faith which the "cult of reassurance" has repudiated as unworthy of the century of the Common Man. The new faith is a positive faith in man's power to have faith and to use it to "conjure up the cooperation of God." It is a confident faith in the latest "prayer techniques" that are guaranteed to get results. It is a streamlined faith in tried and tested spiritual formulas that will bring its adherents their justly deserved prosperity and success.

The critics go on to say that the Peale products and their like are represented as part of a revival or response in Christianity with which they have no valid connection. They influence, mislead, and often disillusion sick, maladjusted, unhappy, or ill-instructed people, obscuring from them Christian realities, it is said. They offer easy comforts, easy solutions to problems and mysteries that sometimes, perhaps, have no comforts or no solutions at all, in glib, worldly terms. They promise a cheap "happiness" in lieu of the joy which Christianity can offer, sometimes in the midst of suffering.

One of America's leading Protestant theologians, Dr. Reinhold Niebuhr, professor of Applied Christianity at Union Theological Seminary in New York, put his objections simply:

> The Christian religion is one of repentance and faith, sin and grace. Christianity stresses the idea that man tends to think more of himself than he should and that there can be no real meeting with God, except through repentance and the confession of sin.
>
> The basic sin of this new cult is its egocentricity. It puts "self" instead of the cross at the center of the picture. Christianity insists that you cannot have faith without repentance, and since the very ideas of sin and repentance are negative, the positive thinkers simply leave them out, or at best, gloss them over. The result is a partial picture of Christianity, a sort of half-truth.[76]

Dr. Niebuhr goes on to explain that the ideas of this new cult are not really new. Historically there has always been at the heart of orthodox Christianity a tendency to corrupt religion sinfully to one's own personal ends. Instead of trying to subordinate one's will to the Divine will, men try to harness Divine power to whatever they want to accomplish. "This new religion of happiness and positive thoughts is the same old heresy. It applies religion to business and personal affairs and embodies the success idea." [77]

Andrew E. Murray, Dean of the Seminary, Lincoln University, Pennsylvania, says:

> The tragedy of Dr. Peale lies in the fact that he gives no help or hope to the individual wrestling with problems beyond his power to solve. In spite of good intentions an individual may be caught in impossible conditions created by society and be unable to do anything about his situation.[78]

Dr. Donald Meyer of Harvard University feels that Dr. Peale's "self-confidence" preaching is of little or no avail to those who feel insecure in the "status-and-money-world" about us. He feels that Dr. Peale blandly ignores the text from the Book of James, that "we are all helpless failures in the last resort." [79]

Dr. Liston Pope, a Congregational minister and Dean of the Yale Divinity School, believes that this kind of religion "represents an attempt at shoring up faltering egos with easy formulas and spiritual gimmicks. But it is too important to be taken lightly," he warns. "This criticism of the new religion of peace of mind is no theological quibble; it is not to be taken in the spirit of a mild difference of opinion between preachers. The peace of mind cult represents a redefinition of the Christian faith and its central themes. That is why it is important for people to see it for what it is." [80]

William Lee Miller, Professor of Religion at Smith College, sums up his views on Dr. Peale as follows:

> It is an idea that has made Dr. Peale. The idea is that affirmative attitudes help to make their own affirmations come true. Dr. Peale takes the obvious, but partial truth in this idea, and builds it into an absolute law; he erects on it a complete and infallible philosophy, psychology, and religion, so that he can solve every problem just by denying it really exists and promises that every wish can be fulfilled just by "thinking" it.[81]

This quest for an easy answer through religion is something Dr. Franklin Clark Fry, President of the United Lutheran Church in America, is also concerned about. Dr. Fry believes that God is being seriously misrepresented by the "positive thinkers." He says, "There is nothing more sinister . . . than the instrumentalization of religion—the use of God to accomplish a specific aim. The true Christian asks, 'What does God want to do through me?' not 'What can He do for me?' " [82]

As Bishop of the Methodist Church for the Washington, D. C. area, Dr. G. Bromley Oxnam said:

> Many of us in the ministry . . . have carried on religion as a routine. We have stood by while Dr. Peale has put drama into his particular kind of religion. I think that by addressing himself to people's needs, he may have been doing some good for certain kinds of people, but I seriously question whether his message is a Christian message. Perhaps the best thing he has done is alert the rest of us to the fact that many of us have been ignoring people's immediate needs in our preaching.
>
> The fundamental weakness of this message is that it is self-centered. . . . Christianity says, "Give thyself." Dr. Peale says, "Help yourself." [83]

Edmund Fuller, the book review editor of *Episcopal Church-news,* writes in the *Saturday Review of Literature:*

> The books and teachings of Pealeism pervert the nature of Christian belief and experience. They make a virtue of being man-centered and self-centered. They seek an immediate, material good. The awesome sense of confrontation with God is gone. The fear of God which is awe has been dispelled. The meaning of worship is nullified and forgotten. God is to be worshipped because he is God. Pealeism and its corollaries debase Christianity to make of it a means to other and lesser ends—which by its nature the Christian religion cannot be.
>
> Where, in all the morass of false witness, whether in quests

for successful living or in saccharine sentimentalist—where are the great, historic central themes, subjects, words of Christianity through the ages? Where are considerations of the Trinity, Incarnation, Covenant, Atonement, Redemption, Salvation, Sin, Offering, Judgment, Worship, Sacrament, Sacrifice, Communion, and the idea of the Holy?

One must say of Pealeism in all its manifestations, paraphrasing Richard Bentley's comment about Pope's translation of Homer, "It is a pretty religion, Mr. Peale, but you must not call it Christianity!" [84]

Some of the criticisms of Dr. Peale's theology stem from sincere intellectual concern. Other criticisms are the result of emotional thinking and rationalization. Often the accusation seems out of proportion to the topic under discussion. The readiness of many of Dr. Peale's critics to accept the notion that he has only a single theme is traceable, in part at least, to the title of his best seller: *The Power of Positive Thinking.* Positive thinking and Dr. Peale have become virtually synonymous. Most of the criticisms of Dr. Peale stem from reading his best seller—few, if any, critics have carefully analyzed the content of his Sunday sermons or his counseling techniques.

The Case In Favor of Dr. Peale

Dr. Peale is aware of the covert and overt criticism of his preaching, and, to some extent, is troubled by it. It is said even by his critics that there is no arrogance in him, no tendency to ignore criticism or brush it aside. An example of this was brought to light recently when Dr. Liston Pope, Dean of the Yale Divinity School, openly attacked the "peace of mind cults." When asked by reporters to comment on the accusations made by Dr. Pope, Dr. Peale replied that the head of a great divinity school must be a sincere, intelligent, and honest man, and that he (Dr. Peale) intended to re-examine his own methods and message in the light of what Dr. Pope had said. If he found that he was deviating in any way from the teaching of the Gospels as he understood them, Dr. Peale told the newsmen, he would try to correct the error.

In defense of his own preaching techniques, Dr. Peale feels that:

> My message is based on my understanding of our Lord's teaching. My methods may seem overpopular to some of the intellectuals of Protestantism, but I feel sometimes they are unable to communicate with ordinary church-going people largely because they reject such methods.[85]

Thus, one of the arguments in favor of Dr. Peale's preaching is that he talks to millions where scholars talk to handfuls. He has given hope to tens of thousands of discouraged, shut-away people. He has reached highly educated people who have for years been missed by the scholarly pronouncements of ordinary clergymen, but who have found a working faith through him.

Those who favor his message say that it is geared to the needs of ordinary man. The great abstractions of religion are diffuse and difficult; most men must be content with less. In an editorial in *The Christian Herald,* Dan Poling, the editor, said:

> It was said of Jesus that the common people heard Him gladly. They heard Him gladly because they could understand Him, because He spoke in the vernacular—the Aramaic, the language of the streets and highways. And the man Peale both lives and talks right down to the grass roots of everyday life, where the common people and all others live and move and have their troubled beings.[86]

Consequently, when Dr. Peale is accused of preaching an oversimplified version of Christianity, one must ask: "Oversimplified for whom?" For the theologian? Perhaps! For the divinity student? Again, perhaps! But the rank and file of humanity, so say his supporters, do not find that his message is oversimplified. If it were, they would not flock to hear him, or to read his books. They would be bored. Therefore, do not find fault with him for not teaching postgraduate courses; he is teaching primary courses, and many more need them than need the postgraduate ones.

In a sermon entitled "Spiritual Snobs," Dr. Samuel M. Shoemaker, minister of the Calvary Episcopal Church in Pittsburgh, made the following remark about Dr. Peale:

> His public addresses and books emphasize—overemphasize, I think—the encouraging and optimistic things about the Christian faith. Heaven knows they are not hard to find! . . . But surely no one can go very far wrong by emphasizing the power of faith, or by thinking that positive outlooks on life are better than negative. Dr. Peale surely does not believe one can be helped without God.[87]

The followers of Dr. Peale also feel that the critics, in their zeal to convict him of oversimplifying and distorting Christianity, are themselves guilty of oversimplifying and distorting. They ignore the qualifications and warnings Dr. Peale gives in order to prove a point in their favor.

A deep interest in psychiatry has characterized Dr. Peale's ministry from the start. He was one of the first churchmen to insist that religion and psychiatry should and could complement each other. In this field of mental health he has his champions as well as his critics. One of his backers is Dr. Newton Bigelow, former Commissioner of the New York State Department of Mental Hygiene, who says:

> It's hard to overestimate the importance of what Dr. Peale has done as a practical preacher using new mass media. His methods have reached many more people than are reached through the usual counseling channels. This I know personally from contacts with many individuals.

Secondly, he has helped to establish psychiatry as a "respectable" branch of medicine, has demonstrated the fact that, in order to help people, psychiatrists and clergymen must often work together and has assisted in putting a little Godliness into the practice of psychiatry.[88]

Even more outspoken is Dr. Smiley Blanton, New York psychiatrist who has worked with Dr. Peale for over twenty-five years. He says that:

Dr. Peale is a great pioneer. He was one of the first men—if not the first—to combine the new science of human behavior known as depth psychology with the discipline of religion. As a result, he has been able to help more people than either religion or depth psychology could help, acting alone.

There are some people who are not helped by his message. But there is no reason why a technique valid for some should be condemned because it doesn't benefit everybody.[89]

Dr. Samuel Cavert, Executive Secretary of the World Council of Churches, said that while he thought Dr. Peale's ideas might have been somewhat "oversold," he had no doubts whatever as to the man's integrity, sincerity or the fact that his ministry was doing a great deal of good.

Writing to a colleague who had expressed unfavorable opinions of Dr. Peale, Dr. T. Christie Innes of the Collingswood Presbyterian Church in Toledo, Ohio, said:

I am all for truth, profundity and breadth in every minister's teaching. But I am as conscientiously opposed to the superficiality of brethren who cannot see and thank God for the good there is in Dr. Peale's presentations, as millions can testify, and see deep enough to forbear the cheap and easy method of lamenting his work because it is not, in their view, all that could be desired. Can we not have Dr. Peale do his great "popular" work, and organize our tremendous theologians to follow up with the "fuller and deeper" insight they profess to have? [90]

In Northampton, Massachusetts, the Reverend Walter C. Couch, Jr., of the Florence Congregational Church, said:

> . . . scarcely a day of full pastoral counseling goes by without someone's telling me just how Norman Vincent Peale's spoken or written words have been a great help in time of trouble or sorrow and my observation is that the help thus received has benefited these people in very wholesome and ethical ways.[91]

There is no doubt that there are thousands—and perhaps millions—of followers of Dr. Peale who have found personal guidance and purpose in his theology. Dr. Peale currently receives about 8000 letters a week. These letters come from every state in the United States as well as countries all over the world. For the most part they are testimonials about how Dr. Peale's books or sermons have given direction, purpose, and meaning to life. In reference to these letters, Grove Patterson, Dr. Peale's former boss, says:

> It seems to me that Norman Vincent Peale is to be measured by the definite results of his speaking and writing. The "Peale Controversy" fades into something pretty unimportant when one reads almost any one of those thousands of letters received at the church or the broadcasting studio or the publisher's office. The lives of uncounted thousands of men and women have been changed by the Peale preaching.[92]

"Theologically I may be unlearned," continues Mr. Patterson, "but I know a religion that works." In a similar vein, Dr. S. Franklin Mack, executive director of the National Council of Churches' Broadcasting and Film Commission, came to Dr. Peale's defense, "It is a constant rebuke to most of us in the leadership of the Christian church today," he said, "that it cannot be said of us as it was of Jesus that 'the common people heard Him gladly.' No evaluation of Dr. Peale can leave out of consideration the rapport he seems to have with people in all walks of life." [93]

In conclusion, in the course of his ministry, Dr. Peale has acquired many friends as well as enemies. His enemies, however, do not seem to direct their criticism at him personally—but rather at his message. Yet at the same time it is difficult to separate the message from the man. For the Peale image is not that of a great orator noted for his eloquent and profound utterings. The Peale image binds the man with his unique message—a message which he has been elaborating from his early preaching career.

But where the critics are concerned, Dr. Peale is willing to concede that perhaps he has made mistakes of emphasis.

> Maybe I have made it all sound too easy . . . That certainly wasn't my intention, because Christianity isn't easy; it's so tough that nobody lives up to it fully. I always tried to emphasize that fact. And maybe I have stressed the tangible, visible rewards of faith too much. But here again, it wasn't because I was trying to appeal to selfishness. It was because I've seen fantastic transformations take place in people who, through self-surrender and the agony of spiritual change, find themselves and become integrated personalities. I've seen these things happen over and over again. I wanted everyone to know about them, to experiment and find out for themselves. . . .
>
> The privilege of reaching great numbers of people with this message is a gift the Lord has given me and I have used it to the utmost of my ability.[94]

Chapter 4

Dr. Peale's
Sermon Themes

Some ministers gain their reputations by applying their religion to the betterment of social conditions. Theodore Parker and Henry Ward Beecher, two famous American ministers of the nineteenth century, might be thought of as falling into this category. Other ministers are known for the beautiful style and imagery of their language. A recent example in this category would be Peter Marshall. Some ministers are known for their scholarship or eloquence. A contemporary example in this case would be Harry Emerson Fosdick.

Dr. Peale, however, did not gain his reputation by delivering eloquent sermons, producing scholarly dissertations, or championing great social causes. Dr. Peale's reputation rose slowly over a lifetime of preaching some unique themes never before popularly allied with Christianity. It is for this reason that this study has chosen to deal mainly with the themes presented in Dr. Peale's sermons. There is no one great sermon which is the key to his success—rather it is the composite of ideas which he has preached over and over again.

In order to analyze the themes of Dr. Peale's sermons it was felt necessary to obtain as many sermons as possible. Some sermons were collected from friends and relatives, while others were received from the Foundation for Christian Living, Pawling, New

York, and from Dr. Peale himself. According to personal correspondence from Mrs. C. C. Peale of the Foundation for Christian
Living; Dr. Peale's personal secretary, Mrs. Mary M. Creighton;
and Dr. Peale himself, this writer has the most complete collec-
tion of sermons that they know to be available. There are 249
sermons, and they date from 1946 to 1960. Sermons given after
1960 are available, but January 1, 1961 was set as the arbitrary
cut-off date for this particular study.

After reading each sermon several times, it was apparent that
certain thematic categories emerged. The problem of establishing
categories involves the extraction of ideas or themes from the
sermons and specifically defining these themes. In this particular
case it was not only necessary to discover, but also to define and
re-define, the indicators for each major category. Accurate definition of both indicators and thematic categories is a prerequisite
to a reliable analysis. The goal, then, is the discovery or selection
of indicators which are completely, accurately, and clearly defined
in relation to both categories and content. The attainment of this
goal is possible only with "the definition and re-definition of indicators, categories, hypotheses, and problems." [95]

In its simplest form the theme is an assertion of the subject
matter. Berelson describes it as "a sentence (or sentence-com-
pound), usually a summary or abstracted sentence, under which a
wide range of specific formulations can be subsumed." [96] The
word "theme" is used interchangeably by many writers with the
terms "assertion," [97] "statement," [98] "proposition," [99] "idea," [100]
"issues," [101] "argument," [102] and "thema." [103]

Irving L. Janis feels that a thematic analysis is one of the most
productive types of content analyses because:

> The "thematic content" corresponds most nearly to the over-all
> signification of a communication. . . . The assertions found in
> a communication are the primary indicators of the intentions

and motives of the communicator. Similarly, the effects which a communication produces on an audience are primarily due to the assertion's content.[104]

Thus we see that the revelation of speaker objectives and the identification of speaker intentions are likely to be revealed in the results of thematic quantification. Since the theme takes the form of an issue, a philosophy or an idea, it is generally regarded as one of the most important units of content analysis.

Some subject matter analyses merely measure the frequency of occurrence of certain themes, and clearly define these themes through the use of synonyms. In such cases a high degree of definitional agreement is obtained. In more complex studies, however, accurate definition is difficult because of a wide variance of opinion concerning connotative or denotative meaning of the indicators. Of utmost importance, then, is the attainment of agreement in definition. Bernard Berelson explains "content analysis stands or falls by its categories . . . A content analysis can be no better than its system of categories." [105] Thus, when the thematic categories were finally formulated to the satisfaction of the author, they were then submitted to a test of reliability. In order for a system of categories to be reliable, they must be arrived at objectively by different analysts. In other words, the term "reliability," as used here, means that "different observers report the same thing." [106] Operating under the same conditions, different coders should arrive at the same conclusions.

Therefore, three independent coders were employed to meet the requirements of reliability. All were college graduates; two had majored in English and one had majored in psychology. These three coders worked with the same selection of six sermons, but at different times and different places. To be reliable, categories must be consistent "among the analysts" as well as "through time." In other words, a single coder or group of coders should arrive at the same results even though a lapse of time occurred between their coding.

The three coders were approached individually by the author and the necessary instructions given. Each coder was asked to note the thematic categories which she felt emerged as she read the six sermons. A list of categories was made by the coder for each sermon read. At the conclusion of this test, the results were compared with the categories arrived at by the author. These results are itemized in Table 1.

TABLE 1. Reliability test
author/coder percentile agreement

SERMON NUMBERS	THEMES PRESENT	CODERS			GROUP RELIABILITY
		1	2	3	
144	12	76%	84%	69%	76%
136	9	88%	100%	100%	96%
137	10	80%	80%	70%	77%
138	8	100%	63%	87%	83%
139	11	90%	100%	100%	97%
132	14	78%	64%	78%	73%
TOTAL	65	85%	82%	84%	84%

The high group reliability percentages are encouraging indications that satisfactory selection, designation, and definition of thematic categories has preceded the coding process. All three coders agreed with the author on an average of more than 80% of the time. This is significant since between 70% and 80% agreement is quite usable in content analysis.[107]

Even though agreement was high as to the designation and definition of categories, the author was able to utilize some of the ambiguities noted by the coders to further define and clarify. Forty-one thematic categories finally emerged as the basic content of the preaching of Dr. Peale. Having attained reliable agreement as to the designation of the separate categories, the investigation could proceed with little doubt as to the validity of its results. Following are the themes which emerged from the preaching of Dr. Peale. As a matter of stylistic preference only, the thematic categories are here placed in the phrase-title form rather than in complete statement form; however, specific form statements and theme-indicator examples are included in their definitions.

1. *The Theme of Action.* "If ye know these things (the will of God), happy are ye if ye do them." The trouble with many people is that they believe in God's power in their lives, but they do not really practice it. When you have a belief that something is right, it is not enough to say, "I believe that." You must live and act according to your belief.

2. *The Theme of Adjustability.* A person's happiness and enjoyment in life is largely dependent upon his ability to adjust to other people and external situations. A person must be able to take things in stride, to make the best of every situation.

3. *The Theme of Beliefs.* It is never necessary to compromise one's beliefs in order to get ahead. A person should be "himself" at all times. He should be directed by his inner convictions, not by external pressures to conform.

4. *The Theme of the Bible.* The Bible provides infallible techniques, formulas, and methodology for dynamic living. It is the most practical book ever written because it answers every question leading to spiritual, physical, and economic success. It is the record of God's truth revealed to man.

5. *The Theme of Christianity.* Christianity is penetrating the life of our time as never before. Not only is it being recognized as a scientific, intelligent, and practical way of thinking and living, but it is recognized as the answer to all the individual, state, and social problems of the world. If you are not a Christian, you are old-fashioned. If you are not a follower of Jesus Christ, you are not in the mode.

6. *The Theme of Death.*   The real person—soul and mind—is not destroyed by what man calls physical death. The present day science of parapsychology offers proof of spiritual life after physical death. Physical death merely destroys the vehicle which has embodied man's personality, soul, and mind while on earth. But man's essence lives on in the "great cloud of witnesses" that touch earthly man's life.

7. *The Theme of Defeat and Fear.*   The accumulation of fears destroys life. Many people are literally crawling through life on their hands and knees. They have no alertness, no snap, no vitality. Cares, fears, difficulties, and troubles have overcome them and they are stumbling through life half-defeated.

8. *The Theme of Dreams, Hopes, Desires.*   All accomplishments, actions, and facts are stimulated first by dreams. These dreams, hopes, and desires are the very roots of creativity. They keep people physically and mentally alive—vivacious, alert, etc. (Dr. Peale is referring here to the conscious visualizing in the mind of some future event—not dreams while sleeping.)

9. *The Theme of the Easy Way.*   The easy way is not to be desired. It will not accomplish anything great. It will not be found in religion. It overlooks the fact that wholeness of life is never achieved by choosing the path of least resistance.

10. *The Theme of Enthusiasm.*   One of the greatest qualities a human being can possess is enthusiasm. It is a spiritual thing. It contributes to a person's success, happiness, and vitality.

11. *The Theme of Faith.*   Faith is available to everyone. It does not make any difference what difficulty you have right now: physical, mental, spiritual, business, or moral; if you will begin to bear upon it the power of faith without doubt, it can be solved. The Bible is filled to overflowing with the truth that faith conquers all, that by faith all things are achieved. The secret, then, of building yourself a better future is to attack it with faith.

12. The Theme of God and Christ. It is through God and Christ that man can achieve wholeness of his mental, physical, spiritual, and emotional faculties. As ruler of all life—whether spiritual or material—God and Christ provide an unending supply of guidance and power. It is through God and Christ that happiness, success, and dynamic living can be achieved.

13. The Theme of the Grace of God. When all else fails, when man has given his all and has not succeeded, the Grace of God is still available to him. No matter how sinful and undeserving we are, the Grace of God makes our approach to God possible.

14. The Theme of Growth. Life means physical as well as spiritual, mental, and emotional growth; and where there is no growth, there is no life; it has subsided, ended. Don't stop growing—don't stand still. Examine your emotions and ideas; if they have begun to crust over, smash them by a spiritual and intellectual renewal. Help them begin to grow once again.

15. The Theme of Our Heritage. The success of our forefathers was due to their love of both freedom and God. American society is decaying because of the rot at its moral roots. It is because so many people no longer know God as intimately as did their fathers.

16. The Theme of Insecurity and Failure. Insecurity and failure are an inevitable result of growing up. As man matures, he learns to readjust to the situations brought on by his failures and insecurities. He learns that a belief and self-confidence in his own ability can help him overcome his insecure feelings and failures. A healthy person learns that inferiority is basically nothing more than disbelief in one's self.

17. The Theme of Interpersonal Relations. The persons we like the best in life are those who bring out the best in us. Similarly, if we make other people like themselves, they in turn will love us. In order to "bring out the best in others," we must strive to be objective, scientific in our relations with them. We must avoid emotionalism and try to understand and accept them for what they are.

18. The Theme of Kindness. Kindness is an old basic law of life that always gains results. Be kind to one another, for kindness works wonders, makes one happy inside, and gives power and delight on the outside.

19. The Theme of the Kingdom of God. The Kingdom of God is within you—within every man. It is God's gift to all humanity—available for the asking.

20. The Theme of Life Goals and Purpose. Life goals and purpose are essential for success. They stimulate dynamic living. Many people fail in life because they have no sense of direction, no system, no guiding principles. They have no major cause or beliefs to give meaning to life. To succeed, man must find a cause and fight for it.

21. The Theme of Love. Love is the greatest healing power known to man. It is the way to get along with other people, enabling man to live as did Jesus. It is the greatest blessing known to producing a normal, healthy life.

22. The Theme of Man. Every man is the unique creation of God, created to live a life characterized by joy, energy, and vitality —to succeed in all areas of life. Man's major concern is "living a better life," and spreading God's message throughout the world.

23. The Theme of Memory. By recalling to mind the beautiful scenes and inspirations of his earlier years, man is able to recharge his spirit and keep his soul alive and vigorous.

24. The Theme of Nature. Learn to notice and appreciate the beauty of nature. The beauty and inspiration of nature are part of God's healing process. It is given by God for every man's enjoyment.

25. The Theme of Politics. Communism will eventually destroy itself because freedom, liberty, and the recognition of God

are essential for sustenance. Any nation built on force and author-
itarianism will perish.

26. *The Theme of Potential Human Power.* Man never fully
realizes his physical, mental, emotional, and spiritual capabilities.
There exist in man powers which can revitalize his life, which
can recharge his spirit and make him into a new man. But few
men are able to develop these God-given powers.

27. *The Theme of Prayer.* Prayer does get results. Properly
utilized, it can revolutionize a person's life. It is the basic method
for problem solving, bringing about guidance, illumination, and
problem solutions. A person who plans his life, and keeps it
planned, according to the instrument of prayer, will achieve the
best aims of life.

28. *The Theme of Problems.* Problems are a normal (essential) part of all life. Greatness stems from meeting and conquering them. If people approach problems in the right frame of
mind, they can always derive some good from them.

Though problems are very real in life, they are not always revealed by a person's outward appearance. A person is often calm
on the outside but chaotic on the inside. Through the help of
God, organizing one's life, and meeting problems head-on, problems can be overcome.

29. *The Theme of Repentance and Housecleaning.* It is never
too late to repent and start anew—to better oneself. Only remember that resentments, ill-will, hatreds, and other hurt feelings
quickly spread and ruin the whole person. Therefore, confess
your failures, mistakes, hatreds, etc., and forget them. Always
move forward. Do not dwell on past disappointments.

30. *The Theme of Revelation and Wisdom.* Wisdom is often
revealed by God in the form of a "sudden thought or inspiration."
It is not always rational and at the time may appear completely
unrelated to what had gone before—an entirely new idea—thus
an inspiration or revelation from God.

31. The Theme of Rhythm of Life. In all life there exists the mountain peaks as well as the valleys, the goods as well as the bads. Periods of "ups" and "downs" are always present. All life has its rhythm. Fulness of life is achieved when life's rhythm is atuned to the rhythm of God.

32. The Theme of Riches. Real riches are not external or material riches. Real riches are spiritual and internal in nature. They are riches that no man can take away.

33. The Theme of Self-Discipline. Nothing really precious in this world is gained without a measure of self-discipline and self-control.

34. The Theme of Solitude. The first step in conquering any problem is to achieve a quiet and peaceful mind. Not only does it help the mind to operate at full capacity, but it is essential for the development of self-confidence. The recognition of God's presence creates the atmosphere of quietness and peacefulness. Thus God is an essential element in solitude.

35. The Theme of Spiritual Living. Spiritual living is the source of real greatness. It provides man with the necessary insight to understand himself and others. Doctors recognize its value in achieving physical and emotional health.

36. The Theme of Stewardship. We must learn to give of our time, talent, and money to others. There is a law of abundance which states that we will receive in proportion to our gifts to others.

The hardest but one of the most rewarding of all gifts is the yearly tithe. This has been a Biblical requirement down through the ages. One-tenth of our income should still be donated to the church in order that we may truly "feel" our giving to God.

37. The Theme of the Subconscious. A person's life can be likened to an iceberg. Seven-eighths of it is always below the surface. Thus it is that defeat or victory depends on one's subconscious attitudes. God presides in the subconscious. Real security flows from the deep founded, inner level of the subconscious. The subconscious is the foundation of our real self.

38. The Theme of Thanksgiving. The attitude of gratitude is important in achieving wholeness in life. Only by enumerating the many blessings bestowed upon us can we fully appreciate the bounty of God.

39. The Theme of Thought and Mind Attitudes. A person's thoughts and attitudes determine the situations of his life. Many illnesses are the result of ill thoughts and attitudes. They are psychosomatic.

Right (true, good) thoughts bring right results. The person whose thoughts are positive gets positive results, whereas the negative thinker leads a negative life characterized by doom, gloom, and failure.

40. The Theme of Truth and Right. The greatest truths in life are all characterized by simplicity. Jesus outranks all the great intellects of the world for one reason: He is able to take the most complicated factors of truth and make them very simple.

41. The Theme of Knowing Yourself. To be successful in daily living, a person must know himself. He should objectively consider his attributes and liabilities and be willing to change his ways. Before a person can know other people and understand the world about him, he must first of all understand and know himself.

As was pointed out earlier, the author was able to use some of the ambiguities noted by the coders to assist him in defining and clarifying the thematic categories. The final list is made up of forty-one categories which were determined by the author. Because of the high group reliability, however, it was not felt necessary to make any systematic adjustments for error and the ultimate categories are not to be thought of as composites.

Chapter

5

The Thematic Analysis

In order to analyze the themes of Dr. Norman Vincent Peale's sermons, several different steps were taken. The purpose of this chapter is merely to state these steps. Chapter 6 will interpret the findings and attempt to relate them to Dr. Peale's life and preaching.

First, a rank order of the themes was prepared (See Appendix, Table 2). The purpose of this rank order of themes was to present the theme occurrences in a progression from the most frequent to the least frequent. The rank order revealed that of the forty-one themes which seem to constitute the basis of the content in Dr. Peale's sermons, seven themes appeared in 50% or more of his sermons. These themes were: (1) The God/Christ Theme, 97%; (2) The Thought Theme, 65%; (3) The Prayer Theme, 63%; (4) The Faith Theme, 58%; (5) The Problem Theme, 57%; (6) The Interpersonal Relations Theme, 50%; and (7) The Defeat/Fear Theme, 50%. This means that seven, or 17%, of Dr. Peale's basic themes occurred in 50% or more of his sermons.

Fourteen themes appeared in 20% to 49% of his sermons and the remaining twenty themes appeared in less than 20% of the sermons. In this last group, eight themes appeared in only 10% of the sermons or less. These eight were: (1) The Kingdom of

God Theme, 10%; (2) The Know Yourself Theme, 10%; (3) The Potential Power Theme, 10%; (4) The Thanksgiving Theme, 9%; (5) The Death Theme, 7%; (6) The Kindness Theme, 7%; (7) The Politics Theme, 5%; and (8) The Riches Theme, 5%.

Since it is only natural that certain themes tend to occur more often in ministers' sermons, the forty-one themes were rated by seven people according to a high or low probability of occurrence scale. For example, if it can be expected that a Protestant minister will talk about God in any given sermon, the God Theme would be marked "high probability of occurrence." On the other hand, it would not necessarily be expected that a minister would talk about baking pies. Thus, the Pie-baking Theme would be marked "low probability of occurrence." Since it was felt that some of the themes might be neutral—i.e., be just as apt to occur as not to occur, a "neutral" column was added. The coders for this exercise were: (1) a housewife, (2) a minister in the Church of Christ, (3) a Methodist minister, (4) a high school teacher, (5) a professor of radio and television, (6) a graduate student in the field of communication theory, and (7) the Assistant Director of the International Cooperation Administration Seminars on Communication. The above seven people knew that Dr. Peale was the minister from whom the themes were taken and also had their forty-one themes titled, i.e., the God/Christ Theme, etc. Since it was felt by the author that this information might have in some way prejudiced their answers, seven students in a Michigan State University graduate readings' course in Speech also performed the task. They, however, were not told where or how the themes had been obtained, and their themes were numbered but not titled. There proved to be no significant difference between the rankings of the two groups.

On the basis of the decisions of these coders, the forty-one themes were divided into three categories: (1) High Probability of Occurrence, (2) Low Probability of Occurrence, and (3) Neutral Probability of Occurrence. Each of the forty-one themes was designated to one of these three categories according to the majority of decisions by the coders. The theme was included in two categories whenever a tie occurred. These three categories of the forty-one themes are presented in Table 3 (see Appendix).

By comparing the ranking of themes in Table 2 with the theme probability of occurrence in Table 3, one can arrive at additional understanding of the themes used by Dr. Peale. For example, the God/Christ Theme occurs in 97% of Dr. Peale's sermons and is also placed in the "High Probability of Occurrence" category most frequently by the coders. Though this finding is significant, it is not as significant as the fact that the Thought Theme, which occurred 65% of the time, was rated by the coders as a "Low Probability of Occurrence" theme. It is the only theme occurring in more than 50% of the sermons analyzed which was given a "Low Probability of Occurrence" rating.

Another step taken to understand in quantitative terms the preaching of Dr. Peale was to study the percentage of occurrence of themes from year to year. This was done to analyze theme trends and the fluency/stability characteristics of the themes. In other words, the author felt it important to know how consistent the themes were over a period of time. Did some themes appear in some years but not in other years? Did a pattern or cycle of themes seem to emerge from year to year? Was there any relationship between themes and certain political or economic factors? Particular attention was paid in this step to the themes with a 50% or higher frequency of occurrence.

The next step taken was to arrange a contingency chart showing the frequency of occurrence of each theme with each other theme. Examples of contingency charts are commonly found on road maps where the distances between major cities are indicated. Since this is a very time-consuming task when done by hand, the themes and their presence or absence in any given sermon were coded for use in Michigan State University's Mystic computer. After the Mystic computer had processed the program, the contingency chart was prepared. This chart was most helpful for two major reasons. First, it provided the analyst with an opportunity to view the inter-relatedness of the various themes. Of particular importance in this respect was the contingency relationship among those themes which appeared in 50% or more of the sermons. For example, out of 249 sermons analyzed, the God/Christ Theme and Thought Theme appeared together in 155, or 62% of the sermons. Out of 249 sermons, the God/Christ and Prayer Themes appeared together in 146, or 59% of the sermons.

The second purpose of the contingency tables was to assist the analyst in performing a linkage analysis of the themes. Linkage analysis is a method of clustering. "It can be used to cluster either people or items, or any objects, for that matter, which have dis-tinctive-cluster characteristics." [108] The result is that every mem-ber of a cluster is more like some other member of that cluster (with respect to the data analyzed) than it is like any member of any other cluster. Thus, each theme in a cluster tends to be more like the other themes in that cluster than like the themes in other clusters.

As a result of the linkage analysis, some interesting relation-ships emerged. The themes of Defeat/Fear, Thought, Interper-sonal Relations, Prayer, and Faith seem to be the major themes around which other themes cluster. The Defeat/Fear Theme is most frequently presented with the themes of Kingdom of God, Insecurity/Failure, Growth, Enthusiasm, and Thought.

The Faith Theme most frequently attracts the themes of Insecurity/Failure, Easy Way, Riches, and Thought.

The Prayer Theme is the major theme in the cluster which includes Truth/Right, Solitude, Grace of God, Dreams, Chris-tianity, Adjustability, and Thought.

The theme of Interpersonal Relations is the cluster focus for the themes of Heritage, Kindness, Memory, Politics, Love and Thought.

It is interesting to note that almost all of the remaining themes as well as the theme clusters relate directly or indirectly to theme 39—the Thought Theme.

In summary, the themes of Dr. Peale were put through the following tests. First, they were arranged in a rank order analysis which enabled the author to determine the most frequently occurring themes. From this chart it is also possible to make inferences concerning the basic theology of Dr. Peale. Second, the forty-one themes were coded by fourteen different people in order that they might be placed in either a high or low probability of occurrence category. The purpose of this was to distinguish those themes which one could expect a Protestant minister to speak about from those themes which one would not expect to hear from a Protestant pulpit. Third, the frequency of occurrence of themes from year to year was studied. This was done to help determine the stability of Dr. Peale's preaching. In essence, did his themes fluctuate from year to year, or were they relatively constant? The next step taken was to prepare a contingency chart showing the frequency of occurrence of each theme with each other theme. This chart enabled the researcher to view the interrelatedness of the various themes. From this step, the final analysis was possible. Using the contingency chart, a linkage analysis was performed on the themes. The linkage analysis enabled the author to conveniently cluster the themes into meaningful relationships. Chapter 6 will now attempt to interpret these findings.

Chapter **6**

Final Evaluations

Chapter 5 merely describes the steps through which the author went in order to analyze the themes of Dr. Peale's sermons. No value statements or interpretations were made in reference to the findings. This chapter will now attempt to interpret these findings and relate them to Dr. Peale's life and preaching.

Seven themes seem to constitute the basis of the preaching of Dr. Norman Vincent Peale. These themes occurred in 50% or more of the sermons used in this study. Six of these themes are general—high probability of occurrence themes which one could expect to hear from any given Protestant pulpit. These six themes are as follows:

1. The God/Christ Theme. This theme had the highest frequency of occurrence; it appeared 97% of the time. Thus, it can be predicted that in most every sermon Dr. Peale will speak about the omniscience, omnipotence, and omnipresence of God. In God and Christ man finds the key to wholeness of his mental, physical, spiritual, and emotional faculties. As the ruler of all life— whether spiritual or material—God and Christ provide an unending supply of guidance and power; and through God and Christ man achieves a state of happiness, success, and dynamic living.

2. The Prayer Theme. The Prayer Theme occurred 63% of the time. Dr. Peale feels that prayer does get results. It is the basic method for problem solving, bringing about guidance, illumination, and solutions. Properly utilized, it can revolutionize a person's life. A person who plans his life, and keeps it planned, according to the instrument of prayer, will achieve the best aims of life.

3. *The Faith Theme.*   This theme occurred in 58% of the sermons. Dr. Peale feels that the secret of building a better future is to attack it with faith. The Bible, he says, is filled to overflowing with the truth that faith conquers all, that by faith all things are achieved. It does not make any difference what difficulty you have right now: physical, mental, spiritual, business, or moral; if you will begin to bear upon it the power of faith without doubt, it can be solved.

4. *The Problem Theme.*   Appearing in 57% of the sermons, this theme defines problems as a normal and essential characteristic of all life. Though on the surface some people appear to have no problems, internally their life is tense and chaotic. Greatness stems from meeting and conquering problems and through the help of God, organizing one's life, and meeting problems head-on they can be overcome.

5. *The Interpersonal Relations Theme.*   The Interpersonal Relations Theme occurred 50% of the time. In this theme Dr. Peale was concerned with getting along with other people. The persons we like the best in life are those who bring out the best in us. Similarly, if we make other people like themselves, they in turn will love us. In order to "bring out the best in others," we must strive to be objective, scientific in our relations with them, and we must avoid emotionalism and try to understand and accept them for what they are.

6. *The Defeat/Fear Theme.*   This theme also occurred in 50% of the sermons. Here Dr. Peale spoke of the fact that many people are literally crawling through life on their hands and knees. The accumulation of fears has destroyed their life. They have no alert-

ness, no snap, no vitality. Cares, fears, difficulties, and troubles have overcome them and they are stumbling through life half-defeated.

The six themes just discussed, then, are themes which do not necessarily distinguish Dr. Peale from any other Protestant minister. They are themes which one could expect to hear from any Protestant pulpit. What is significant is that Dr. Peale has chosen to speak on these themes at least 50% or more of the time. Because of this emphasis on the part of Dr. Peale, it can be assumed that these six themes play a major role in his theology.

The second most frequently occurring theme was the Thought Theme. This theme occurred in 65% of the sermons read and was rated as a specific-low probability of occurrence theme by the coders. This high percentage of occurrence of a theme which is not necessarily thought of as a typical ministerial theme would appear to differentiate Dr. Peale from the average Protestant minister. In other words, this theme, which constitutes one of the basic messages of Dr. Peale's sermons, appears to be different from themes which one might expect to hear in a typical Protestant church. This theme is the message that thoughts and mind attitudes determine the situation of a person's life. Thus, a person becomes what he "thinks." The person whose thoughts are positive gets positive results, whereas the negative thinker leads a negative life characterized by doom, gloom, and failure.

Through the process of linkage analysis, the Thought Theme emerges as the main cluster focal point. No matter what other theme is introduced, this idea is either directly or indirectly related to it. The Thought Theme appears to be the most outstanding and significant characteristic of Dr. Peale's preaching. He finds a tremendous source of energy in the psychological concept of positive thinking—a source of energy which could realign the direction of the soul and bring purpose and meaning to a troubled life.

The theme is nothing new or original with Dr. Peale. The Bible tells us that "As a man thinketh, so is he." The great Stoic philosopher, Marcus Aurelius, said: "Our life is what our thoughts make it." Ralph Waldo Emerson felt that "A man is what he thinks about all day long." In the more modern world, Menninger insisted that "Attitudes are more important than facts." The voice of William James instructed mankind that "The greatest discovery of my generation is that human beings can alter their lives by altering their attitudes of mind." Dr. Peale read frequently from the works of these great men, but in his searching and reading of psychiatric literature he came across a sentence that seemed to state these principles even more explicitly: "In physics, the basic factor is force, in psychiatry, the basic factor is the realizable wish." [109]

It is around this concept of the "realizable wish" that Dr. Peale molds his sermons. He feels that the mind cannot directly control the circumstances that surround it. But it can control the attitudes of the individual to such circumstances. Since the most effective mind conditioner known to man is religion, so Dr. Peale feels, it is only natural to make use of religion to change attitudes and, ultimately, circumstances.

> With God's help you can do amazing things in your life if you want to do so with all your heart, which means with all of your deep desire and real faith. You are master of your life—God and you.[110]

Thus, for Dr. Peale, success or lack of success depends largely on the condition of a man's mind. He cites example after example that the basic teachings of Christianity—love, kindness, unselfishness, and service—are stronger than negative thoughts. A positive thought implanted in the mind, such as love or kindness, can drive out negative thoughts and keep them out.

The following example is cited as an illustration of Dr. Peale's philosophy at work. After a sermon preached at the Marble Collegiate Church, an elder of the church came forward and said to Dr. Peale:

> That was an interesting sermon, Doctor . . . Very interesting. I'm sure a lot of the congregation went away feeling quite pleased with themselves. But tell me—is that really the function of the pulpit, to remind people of how good they are? I should have thought it was just the reverse, to remind them of their shortcomings, the need for change, the necessity for improvement.

Dr. Peale's reply was:

> There's evil in all of us as well as good. I know that, and from time to time I will say so. But I think God wants His children to live fully and gladly. People can't be effective if they're frightened and discouraged.

To this the elder replied:

> They won't be better people if they lose their humility. In effect, this morning, you were counseling those people to lift themselves by their own bootstraps. It can't be done. Wishing won't get an unemployed man a job.

Dr. Peale replied again:

> No, . . . wishing won't. But confidence often will. Unless a man believes in himself, nobody else is going to believe in him. If a man has lost faith in himself, it won't help him much if I stand up in the pulpit and tell him that he's a miserable worm . . ." [111]

Dr. Peale was once again voicing the opinion of the great psychologist and philosopher, William James: "Believe that you possess significant reserves of health, energy and endurance, and your belief will help create the fact." [112]

It is because Dr. Peale has placed just such importance on the

Thought Theme that he has been attacked by many critics. Most of the critics say that he has subordinated God to the will of man. He has made man the complete master of his fate. Apparently the critics are overlooking the total message of Dr. Peale, however, for in 62% of the sermons studied, the Thought Theme and the God/Christ Theme are both discussed together. Although the Thought Theme is the focal point of his message, it is not presented in isolation, but only integrated with other themes which are a part of the more usual Christian message. However, since the Thought Theme distinguishes Dr. Peale from other contemporary Protestant ministers and is representative of a somewhat unique approach to religion, the critics have aimed their fire in that direction.

Dr. Peale feels that preachers everywhere could have larger congregations if they gave more attention to teaching a practical, workable message. He feels that the minister of today must not only be a businessman but a scientist in his own right—a therapist who applies spiritual and psychological truths in helping people to adjust in a healthful and creative manner to the life of this world.

Thus, Dr. Peale has adapted Christianity to meet the needs of this world as he sees them. As a result, he has placed great emphasis on the solving of problems. His sermons are nearly 100% problem-solving sermons. They do not deal with the dogma and doctrine of the church. In order to sell religion he feels that the minister must describe his product in easily understandable terms and make it meet the customer's needs and deep desires. It is to this end that he directs his attention. A subject is important only if it has direct, immediate, and practical usage for the members of his congregation. Therefore, practically all of Dr. Peale's themes can be tied directly to the solving of problems. A quick review of the titles of some of his sermons will reveal the nature of these problems: "How to Overcome Anxiety," "How to Combat Fear," "How to Stop Worrying," etc.

By analyzing the results of the linkage analysis, it appears that each one of the clusters has a negative-positive or problem-solution aspect. This problem-solution quality is inherent in the clusters. Also, the focal point of the cluster is in some way amplified, intensified, or clarified by its surrounding themes. The Defeat/Fear Theme is a focal point theme and presents a problem which many people face. The surrounding themes give the answer to this problem. For example: In order to overcome a feeling of defeat and fear, a person must accept the Kingdom of God which is available to him; grow physically, spiritually, and emotionally; understand that insecurity and failure are a normal process of growing up; become enthusiastic about the life around him by changing his thoughts and mind attitudes to a positive rather than a negative nature. Also, faith comes when a person seeks to understand, accept, and believe in himself; when a person forgoes the easy, worldly way and puts his emphasis on the development of spiritual riches; and when a person changes his negative thoughts to positive ones.

In telling how to overcome a problem, Dr. Peale presents specific techniques, methods, and formulas. He feels that by earnestly and sincerely attempting to find the will of God, and a stronger foundation for faith, people will necessarily have to eliminate their wrongdoing, and undergo a self-examination for traces of the pride, envy, malice, or hatred that blocks the flow of spiritual power. He feels that this power is present—available to all people. Christianity, he says, is a dynamic religion. It works—when it is worked. Simply put, Dr. Peale declares that belief in God, if it is not instinctive, can be acquired by working for it. For this reason he tries to tell exactly what work is necessary to obtain belief in God. He presents his explanation of how to overcome a problem and documents it with many personal examples of friends who have tried his methods and have succeeded. His examples speak freely of the material as well as spiritual rewards they receive. Though he is often criticized for his emphasis of the material rewards, he says he does not refer to them through selfishness, but because "I've seen fantastic transformations take place in people. . . ." [113]

Man does play an important role in Dr. Peale's preaching. Dr. Peale's appeal to self-interest is strong, and some of the promises made seem large. Apparently Dr. Peale accepts at face value the statement of Jesus: "If you have faith, nothing shall be impossible unto you." He believes that Jesus meant exactly what he said—literally, factually, and completely.

Even though Dr. Peale's fame has spread greatly and achieved its peak since 1946, this success cannot be attributed to his introduction of new themes, ideas, or philosophies. Rather, it can be attributed to the fact that his message has been slowly and steadily disseminated via mass communication throughout the country. Dr. Peale's message has not changed to any marked degree in the last 14 years. He is preaching today on the same themes he used in the late 1940's, and the frequency of their usage is relatively the same. The man became associated with an idea and with the acceptance of the idea came also the success of the man.

Although the following observations are not directly a part of this study, it is perhaps of interest to relate some additional points concerning Dr. Peale's sermons. For example, it appears that Dr. Peale took to heart the early advice given him by Grove Patterson and his father. His over-all sentence structure seems to be direct and simple and the words are assembled and related so as to convey thought with an economy of effort. The sentences are short but do not suffer from a choppy or staccato pattern. Other than its shortness, Dr. Peale's sentence structure is best characterized by a "normality" or "well-roundedness," since there appear to be no outstanding features which call attention to themselves.

"Simplicity" is the key descriptive word in this discussion of his style. His sentences appear to be designed to communicate thought, and there is little or no embellishment that might get in the way. The use of simile, metaphor, alliteration, hyperbole, and allegory is kept at a minimum. On one occasion, after a sermon, a member of the congregation came forward and asked why Dr. Peale had made no reference to the Blood of the Lamb. Dr. Peale countered by asking just what the man meant by the Blood of the Lamb. The man said he didn't know, but that all the good preachers he had ever heard talked about it. Dr. Peale's reply was:

> Look, . . . I know what is meant by the Blood of the Lamb, even if you don't. The reason I don't use the old religious terminology is that most of my listeners wouldn't understand it any more than you do. There wouldn't be much point in my getting up there and talking to them in French or German, would there? I try to use language and ideas that every person in my audience can understand.[114]

Perhaps the outstanding characteristic of his style is his extensive use of the illustration. It would be safe to say that his illustrative material usually consumes from one-third to two-thirds of his text. For the most part his illustrations are drawn out of his own personal experience. He feels that the minister should be able to justify everything he says in the pulpit through laboratory experience. "I'm afraid of theoretical stuff in that field. You haven't any right to fool around with theory there." [115] His illustrations are down to earth, homey illustrations used mainly for expository purposes in an effort to amplify, intensify, and clarify. "I preach out of my yesterdays," he once said to a friend. He feels that people like this; that not only do they recognize the ring of authenticity, but also they are reminded of similar experiences in their own lives. In order to make the illustrations as effective as possible, he weaves into the story elements of history, human interest, bits of dialogue, and humor.

It can be said, then, that Dr. Peale's style is a personal one, directed in a conversational language to his congregation. It is simple, direct, concise, and unadorned.

In summary, this rhetorical and thematic analysis of the preaching of Dr. Peale has accomplished the following: (1) It has attempted to trace the development and growth of Dr. Peale as a public speaker and preacher. In the biographical section the philosophy of Dr. Peale concerning speech making was also presented.

It can be concluded from this analysis that Dr. Peale's message is not inconsistent with his background. Even a very selective study of his biography readily reveals the influence of both a severely Protestant (Methodist) upbringing, and the influence of much contact with the world and its problems. Dr. Peale's theology is not unexpected, then, nor is his concern for human beings. Neither is his showmanship, nor even his unquestioned ability as a speaker and writer, for these aspects of his life and personality are also reflected in his biography.

(2) It has presented both favorable and unfavorable comment concerning Dr. Peale, raising the question which the later thematic analysis was designed to answer.

(3) It has analyzed the sermon themes in detail, identifying seven themes used by Dr. Peale in 50% or more of the sermons considered. In addition, when analyzed over a fourteen-year period, these seven themes were found to remain relatively constant from year to year. Thus, it can be said that Dr. Peale has consistently presented his point of view throughout the entire period, 1946–1960.

The one characteristic theme which seems to differentiate Dr. Peale's preaching from that of other Protestant ministers is his emphasis of what has been called the Thought Theme. Linkage analysis has shown that, although the Thought Theme is the focal point of his message, it is not presented in isolation, but only integrated with other themes which are a part of the more usual Christian message.

One important question to ask is: Did the critics of Dr. Peale become so biased by his presentation of the Thought Theme that they overlooked the other six themes which occurred with it? In other words, did their expectation of what a Protestant minister should preach become so disrupted by the introduction of the alien Thought Theme that they could no longer detect the conservative theology of the other six themes which occurred in more than 50% of his sermons? Many people clearly think of Dr. Peale as presenting only one-theme-sermons (the "power of positive thinking") and a ready implication is that the introduction of an idea beyond the limits of their expectation caused a bias to enter into their perception.

This study, then, has taken a minister with a controversial public image as reflected largely in print, and has sought through a quantitative thematic analysis to reject or confirm the public image. The main conclusion is that the public image is essentially correct, but only up to a point. In other words, although his critics tend to isolate the ideas contained in his Thought Theme, Dr. Peale does not. In his sermons the Thought Theme is never presented in isolation, but is consistently embedded in what can only be described as a primarily conservative Protestant theology.

Appendix

TABLE 2. Rank order of themes

THEME		THEMATIC OCCURRENCE	
TITLE	RANK	TIMES APPEARED	PERCENTAGE[a]
God/Christ	1	242	97%
Thought	2	164	65
Prayer	3	156	63
Faith	4	145	58
Problems	5	143	57
Interpersonal Relations	6	125	50
Defeat/Fear	7	125	50
Action	8	114	46
Repentance/Housecleaning	9	104	42
Love	10	98	39
Man	11	98	39
Christianity	12	94	38
Potential Power	13	92	37
Bible	14	86	35
Spiritual Life	15	85	34
Truth/Right	16	67	27
Revelation/Wisdom	17	65	26
Insecurity/Failure	18	63	25
Rhythm of Life	19	63	25
Solitude	20	58	23
Dreams	21	53	21
Beliefs	22	46	18
Subconscious	23	45	18
Goals/Purpose	24	39	16
Enthusiasm	25	38	15
Growth	26	38	15
Memory	27	33	13
Adjustability	28	33	13
Stewardship	29	32	13

[a] Figured on possible 249 sermons

TABLE 2.   Rank order of themes (*cont.*)

| THEME | | THEMATIC OCCURRENCE | |
TITLE	RANK	TIMES APPEARED	PERCENTAGE[a]
Heritage	30	30	12
Easy Way	31	29	12
Nature	32	29	12
Grace of God	33	28	11
Self-Discipline	34	26	10
Know Yourself	35	25	10
Kingdom of God	36	25	10
Thanksgiving	37	22	9
Death	38	17	7
Kindness	39	17	7
Politics	40	12	5
Riches	41	12	5

TABLE 3. Theme placement in probability of occurrency category

| THEME | PROBABILITY OF OCCURRENCE | | |
	HIGH	LOW	NEUTRAL
1. Action	x		
2. Adjustability			x
3. Beliefs			x
4. Bible	x		
5. Christianity	x		
6. Death	x		
7. Defeat/Fear	x		
8. Dreams			x
9. Easy Way	x		
10. Enthusiasm			x
11. Faith	x		
12. God/Christ	x		
13. Grace of God	x		
14. Growth	x		
15. Heritage	x		
16. Insecurity/Failure		x	
17. Interpersonal Relations	x		
18. Kindness	x		
19. Kingdom of God	x		
20. Goals/Purpose	x		
21. Love	x		
22. Man	x		
23. Memory		x	
24. Nature	x		
25. Politics			x
26. Potential Power			x
27. Prayer	x		
28. Problems	x		
29. Repentance/Housecleaning	x		
30. Revelation/Wisdom	x		
31. Rhythm of Life	x		
32. Riches	x		
33. Self-Discipline	x		
34. Solitude	x		
35. Spiritual Life	x		
36. Stewardship	x		
37. Subconscious		x	
38. Thanksgiving	x		
39. Thought		x	
40. Truth/Right	x		
41. Know Yourself	x		

Footnotes

[1] Norman Vincent Peale, "Enthusiasm Will Do Wonders for You," *Sermon Publications,* V, No. 11 (May 10, 1953), p. 1.

[2] Arthur Gordon, *Norman Vincent Peale: Minister to Millions* (New Jersey: Prentice-Hall, Inc., 1958), p. 21.

[3] *Ibid.,* p. 19.

[4] *Ibid.*

[5] *Ibid.,* p. 34.

[6] Norman Vincent Peale, "Look Big at Life," *Sermon Publications,* VII, No. 5 (September 25, 1955), p. 9.

[7] Arthur Gordon, *op. cit.,* p. 21.

[8] Norman Vincent Peale, "The Happiest Day of Your Life," *Sermon Publications,* III, No. 9 (February 24, 1952), pp. 9–10.

[9] Arthur Gordon, *op. cit.,* p. 21.

[10] *Ibid.,* p. 27.

[11] *Ibid.*

[12] *Ibid.*

[13] *Ibid.*

[14] *Ibid.,* p. 24.

[15] Eugene White and Clair Henderlider, "What Norman Vincent Peale Told Us About His Speaking," *The Quarterly Journal of Speech,* XL (December, 1954), p. 406.

[16] Arthur Gordon, *op. cit.,* p. 36.

[17] *Ibid.*

[18] Eugene White and Clair Henderlider, *loc. cit.,* p. 408.

[19] Arthur Gordon, *op. cit.,* p. 50.

[20] Eugene White and Clair Henderlider, *loc. cit.,* p. 409.

[21] Norman Vincent Peale, "What to Do When You Are Criticized," *Sermon Publications,* IX, No. 12 (December 8, 1957), p. 9.

[22] Arthur Gordon, *op. cit.,* p. 53.

[23] *Ibid.*

[24] *Ibid.,* p. 62.

[25] *Ibid.,* p. 60.

[26] Eugene White and Clair Henderlider, *loc. cit.,* p. 409.

[27] Arthur Gordon, *op. cit.,* p. 69.

[28] *Ibid.*

[29] Eugene White and Clair Henderlider, *loc. cit.*, p. 409.

[30] Arthur Gordon, *op. cit.*, p. 70.

[31] *Ibid.*, p. 78.

[32] *Ibid.*

[33] Norman Vincent Peale, "Lose Your Fears Through Faith," *Sermon Publications*, IV, No. 27 (April 26, 1953), p. 7.

[34] Norman Vincent Peale, "Why I Preach as I Do," *Christian Herald*, LXXIX, No. 1 (January, 1956), pp. 65–66.

[35] *Ibid.*, p. 66.

[36] *Ibid.*

[37] Arthur Gordon, *op. cit.*, p. 86.

[38] *Ibid.*, p. 87.

[39] *Ibid.*, p. 89.

[40] *Ibid.*, p. 91.

[41] Eugene White and Clair Henderlider, *loc. cit.*, p. 409.

[42] *Ibid.*, pp. 409–410.

[43] Arthur Gordon, *op. cit.*, pp. 105–106.

[44] Norman Vincent Peale, "Why I Preach as I Do," *loc. cit.*, p. 34.

[45] Norman Vincent Peale, "God's Help Is Available to You," *Christian Herald*, LXXIX, No. 2 (February, 1956), p. 34.

[46] *Ibid.*

[47] *Ibid.*

[48] Arthur Gordon, *op. cit.*, p. 145.

[49] *Ibid.*, p. 155.

[50] Norman Vincent Peale, "The Kind of Preaching That Matters," *Reader's Digest*, LXVIII (May, 1956), p. 36.

[51] Eugene White and Clair Henderlider, *loc. cit.*, pp. 410–411.

[52] Arthur Gordon, *op. cit.*, p. 178.

[53] Frank S. Mead, "Down-to-Earth Gospel and Modern Science Clasp Hands and Change Lives on New York's Rich Fashionable Fifth Avenue," *Grassroots in Manhattan* (Foundation For Christian Living: Pawling, New York).

[54] *Ibid.*

[55] Norman Vincent Peale, "God's Help Is Available to You," *loc. cit.*, p. 67.

[56] *Ibid.*

[57] *Ibid.*, p. 71.

[58] Arthur Gordon, *op. cit.*, p. 241.

[59] *Ibid.*, p. 192.

[60] Arthur Gordon, *op. cit.*, p. 179.

61 Eugene White and Clair Henderlider, *loc. cit.*, p. 414.
62 Norman Vincent Peale, "Self-Confidence Can Be Yours," *Sermon Publications*, III, No. 22 (February 17, 1952), p. 11.
63 Eugene White and Clair Henderlider, *loc. cit.*, p. 411.
64 *Ibid.*, p. 412.
65 *Ibid.*
66 *Ibid.*, p. 413.
67 *Ibid.*
68 *Ibid.*
69 *Ibid.*, p. 415.
70 Phyllis Cerf, "Norman Vincent Peale's First Job," *Good Housekeeping* (July, 1958), p. 94.
71 Arthur Gordon, *op. cit.*, p. 227.
72 "The Campaign," *Time Magazine*, LXXVI, No. 12 (September 19, 1960), p. 21.
73 Norman Vincent Peale, "The Kind of Preaching that Matters," *loc. cit.*, p. 36.
74 William Peters, "The Case Against 'Easy' Religion," *Redbook*, CV, No. 5 (September, 1955), p. 22.
75 *Ibid.*
76 *Ibid.*, pp. 22, 92.
77 *Ibid.*, p. 22.
78 Andrew E. Murray, "Correspondence," *The Reporter*, XII (February 24, 1955), p. 12.
79 Dr. Donald Meyer, "The Confidence Man," *New Republic*, CXXXIII (July 11, 1955), p. 10.
80 William Peters, *loc. cit.*, p. 92.
81 William Lee Miller, "Some Negative Thinking About Norman Vincent Peale," *Reporter*, XII (January 13, 1955), p. 20.
82 William Peters, *loc. cit.*, p. 93.
83 *Ibid.*
84 Edmund Fuller, "Pitchmen in the Pulpit," *Saturday Review of Literature*, XL (March 9, 1957), pp. 29–30.
85 Arthur Gordon, "The Case for 'Positive' Faith," *Redbook*, CV (September, 1955), p. 25.
86 Arthur Gordon, *Minister to Millions, op. cit.*, p. 256.
87 Arthur Gordon, "The Case For 'Positive' Faith," *loc. cit.*, p. 24.
88 *Ibid.*, p. 94.
89 *Ibid.*, p. 25.
90 *Ibid.*, p. 96.
91 *Ibid.*

[92] Grove Patterson, "What Motivates Peale's Critics?" *Christian Herald,* LXXIX, No. 1 (January, 1956), p. 79.

[93] "Issue of Dr. Peale," *Newsweek,* XLV (February 21, 1955), p. 86.

[94] Arthur Gordon, *Minister to Millions, op. cit.,* pp. 253–254.

[95] Bernard Berelson, *Content Analysis in Communication Research* (New York: American Book-Stratford Press, Inc., 1952), pp. 163–164.

[96] *Ibid.,* p. 138.

[97] Nathan C. Leites and Ithiel de Sola Pool, *On Content Analysis* (Washington: Library of Congress, Experimental Division for Study of Wartime Communications, No. 26, 1942), cited by Bernard Berelson, *ibid.,* p. 138.

[98] *Ibid.*

[99] Lasswell and Associates, "The Politically Significant Content of the Press Coding Procedures," *Journalism Quarterly,* XIX (March, 1942), pp. 12–13.

[100] Ernst Kris and Hans Speier, *German Radio Propaganda* (Oxford: Oxford University Press, 1944), p. 41.

[101] Douglas Wables and Bernard Berelson, *What the Voters Were Told: An Essay in Content Analysis* (University of Chicago: Graduate Library School, 1941), cited by Bernard Berelson, *op. cit.,* p. 138.

[102] *Ibid.*

[103] Irvin L. Child, Elmer H. Potter and Estelle M. Levine, "Children's Textbooks and Personality Development: An Exploration in the Social Psychology of Education," *Psychological Monographs,* IX, No. 3 (1946), p. 3.

[104] Irving L. Janis, "The Problem of Validating Content Analysis," *Language of Politics,* eds. H. Lasswell, N. Leites and Associates (New York: The Cornwall Press, Inc., 1949), p. 57.

[105] Bernard Berelson, *op. cit.,* p. 147.

[106] Irving L. Janis, "The Problem of Validating Content Analysis," *op. cit.,* p. 56.

[107] Harold D. Lasswell, Daniel Lerner and Ithiel de Sola Pool, *The Comparative Study of Symbols* (Stanford: Stanford University Press, 1952), p. 62.

[108] Louis L. McQuitty, "Elementary Linkage Analysis for Isolating Orthogonal and Oblique Types and Typal Relevancies," *Educational and Psychological Measurement,* XVII (1957), pp. 207–229.

109 Arthur Gordon, *Minister to Millions, op. cit.,* p. 228.

110 Norman Vincent Peale, "Are We Using the Power God Has Given Us?" *Reader's Digest,* LXXI (September, 1957), p. 130.

111 Arthur Gordon, *Minister to Millions, op. cit.,* p. 159.

112 Norman Vincent Peale, "Priceless Power of Enthusiasm," *Reader's Digest,* LXXII (March, 1958), p. 36.

113 Arthur Gordon, *op. cit.,* pp. 253–254.

114 *Ibid.,* p. 252.

115 Lewis Nichols, "Talk With Dr. Peale," *New York Times Book Review Section,* October 31, 1954, p. 18.

Bibliography

BOOKS

Berelson, Bernard. *Content Analysis in Communication Research*. New York: American Book-Stratford Press, Inc., 1952.

Gordon, Arthur. *Minister to Millions*. Englewood Cliffs, New Jersey: Prentice-Hall, Inc., 1958.

Kris, Ernst, and Speier, Hans. *German Radio Propaganda*. Oxford: Oxford University Press, 1944.

Lasswell, H., Leites, N., and Associates. *Language of Politics*. New York: The Cornwall Press, Inc., 1949.

Lasswell, Harold, Lerner, Daniel, and de Sola Pool, Ithiel. *The Comparative Study of Symbols*. Stanford: Stanford University Press, 1952.

Miller, James Grier (ed.) *Experiments in Social Process: A Symposium on Social Psychology*. New York: McGraw-Hill Book Company, Inc., 1950.

Peale, Norman Vincent. *A Guide to Confident Living*. New York: Prentice-Hall, Inc., 1948.

_____. *Stay Alive All Your Life*. Englewood Cliffs, New Jersey: Prentice-Hall, Inc., 1957.

_____. *The Art of Living*. New York: The Abingdon Press, 1937.

_____, and Smiley Blanton. *The Art of Real Happiness*. New York: Prentice-Hall, Inc., 1950.

_____. *The Power of Positive Thinking*. New York: Prentice-Hall, Inc., 1952.

ARTICLES

Adcock, C. J. "A Note on Cluster-Directed Analysis," *Psychometrika*, XVII (1952), pp. 249–253.

Cattell, R. B. "A Note on Correlation Clusters and Cluster Search Methods," *Psychometrika*, IX (1944), pp. 169–184.

Cerf, Phyllis, "Norman Vincent Peale's First Job," *Good Housekeeping* (July, 1958), p. 94.

"Doctor Peale: An Articulate Leader of Christianity," *Newsweek,* XLII (December 28, 1953), pp. 43–45.

Fuller, Edmund. "Pitchmen in the Pulpit," *Saturday Review of Literature,* XL (March, 1957), pp. 29–30.

Gordon, Arthur. "The Case For 'Positive' Faith," *Redbook,* CV (September, 1955), p. 25.

Hamilton, Thomas. "Social Optimism and Pessimism in American Protestantism," *Public Opinion Quarterly,* VII (1942), pp. 280–283.

"Issue of Dr. Peale," *Newsweek,* XLV (February 21, 1955), pp. 86 ff.

Lasswell, H., and Associates. "The Politically Significant Content of the Press: Coding Procedures," *Journalism Quarterly,* XIX (March, 1942), pp. 12–13.

McQuitty, L. L. "Agreement Analysis: Classifying Persons by Predominant Patterns of Responses," *British Journal of Statistical Psychology,* IX (1956), pp. 5–16.

_____. "Elementary Linkage Analysis for Isolating Orthogonal and Oblique Types and Typal Relevancies," *Educational and Psychological Measurement,* XVII (1957), pp. 207–229.

Mead, Frank S. "Down-to-Earth Gospel and Modern Science Clasp Hands and Change Lives on New York's Rich Fashionable Fifth Avenue," *Grassroots in Manhattan.* New York: Foundation for Christian Living.

Meyer, Dr. Donald. "The Confidence Man," *New Republic,* CXXXIII (July 11, 1955), pp. 10 ff.

Miller, William Lee. "Some Negative Thinking About Norman Vincent Peale," *Reporter,* XII (January 13, 1955), pp. 20 ff.

_____, and J. Monahan. "Pastor of Troubled Souls," *Reader's Digest,* LXIV (February, 1954), pp. 65–69.

"Minister to Millions," *Look,* XVII (September 22, 1953), pp. 86–91.

"New One by Dr. Peale," *Newsweek,* IL (March 18, 1957), p. 124.

Nichols, Lewis. "Talk With Dr. Peale," *New York Times Book Review Section* (October 31, 1954), p. 18.

"Pastors Raise Church Issue Here," *Washington Post-Times Herald,* (September 8, 1960), p. 1.

Patterson, Grove. "What Motivates Peale's Critics?" *Christian Herald,* LXXIX (January, 1956), pp. 24 ff.

Peale, Norman Vincent. "Are We Using the Power God Has Given Us?" *Reader's Digest.* LXXI (September, 1957), p. 130.

Peale, Norman Vincent. "Beyond Death There Is Life," *Reader's Digest*, LXXI (October, 1957), pp. 88–90.

_____. "God's Help Is Available to You," *Christian Herald*, LXXIX (February, 1956), pp. 32 ff.

_____. "Priceless Power of Enthusiasm," *Reader's Digest*, LXXII (March, 1958), pp. 35–38.

_____. "The Kind of Preaching That Matters," *Reader's Digest*, LXVIII (May, 1956), pp. 33–37.

_____. "Why I Preach as I Do," *Christian Herald*, LXXIX (January, 1956), pp. 24–25.

"Peale Offers to Resign Over 'Unwise' Actions," *The Washington Post-Times Herald* (September 19, 1960), p. A-12.

Peters, William. "The Case Against 'Easy' Religion," *Redbook*, CV (September, 1955), pp. 22 ff.

"The Campaign," *Time Magazine*, LXXVI (September 19, 1960), pp. 21 ff.

"Tranquilizers in Print," *Time*, LXIX (March 25, 1957), pp. 112–118.

White, Eugene B., and Henderlider, Clair. "What Norman Vincent Peale Told Us About His Speaking," *Quarterly Journal of Speech*, XI (December, 1954), pp. 407–416.

SERMONS

Peale, Norman Vincent. Pawling, New York: Foundation for Christian Living.

1946, "How to Make 1947 a Great Year"
1947, "A Sure Answer for All Your Problems"
    "The Art of Being Popular"
    "It's Amazing How Wonderful Life Can Be"
    "How to Change Unsatisfactory Situations"
    "You Can Rise Above Every Failure"
    "How to Be an Interesting Personality"
    "Try Kindness—It Works Wonders"
    "We Have Not Lost Those Who Have Died"
1948, "Living at Peace With Yourself and Others"
    "Techniques for Solving Your Personal Problems"
    "Don't Stumble Through Life Half Defeated—Live With Power"
    "You Can Achieve Your Cherished Hopes"
    "Method for Getting Over Hurt Feelings"

"Prescription for Heartache"
"Never Think of Yourself as Beaten"
"How to Successfully Meet a Crisis"
"Whatever You Do, Don't Stop Growing"
"The Greatest Thing in This Country"
1949, "Live With Anticipation, Not Apprehension"
III, Nos. 3, 7, 18–24, 27, 31, 33;
IV, Nos. 2, 5, 8, 10–11, 15–21, 23, 26–27, 31–32;
V, Nos. 2–3, 5–6, 8–16, 18–24, 26–32;
VI, Nos. 1–5, 8–20, 22–30, 32–35;
VII, Nos. 1–32;
VIII, Nos. 2–27;
IX, Nos. 1–28;
X, Nos. 1–29;
XI, Nos. 1–27.